LEARNING WORKS ENRICHMENT SERIES

ADVERTISING
COMMUNICATION
ECONOMICS

WRITTEN BY DIANE SYLVESTER
ILLUSTRATED BY BEVERLY ARMSTRONG

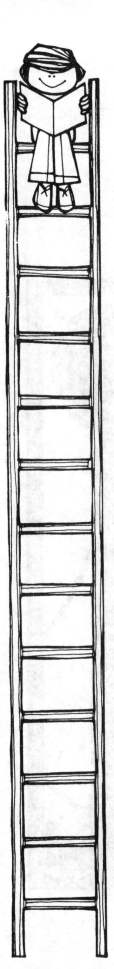

The Learning Works

Contents

To the Teacher 5–6

Advertising 7–30
Bulletin Board Ideas 8
Learning Center Ideas 9
Pretest 10
What Is Advertising? 11
Early Advertisements 12
Early Advertisements Activity Sheet 13
Advertising in America 14–15
Outdoor Advertising 16
Futuristic Outdoor Ads 17
Magazine Advertising 18
Techniques Used in Magazine Advertising 19
Television Commercials 20
Hookers and Grabbers 21
Identifying Types of Television Commercials 22–23
Propaganda 24
Subliminal Advertising 25
Advertising Regulations 26
Correlated Activities 27–28
Answer Key 28
Posttest 29
Advertising Executive Award 30

Communication 31–73
Bulletin Board Ideas 32
Learning Center Ideas 33
Pretest 34
Communication Time Line 35–37
What Is Communication? 38
Communication Diagram 39
From Stone to Paper 40–41
The Evolution of Language 42
The Evolution of Language Activity Sheet 43
Ninety-Two Ways to Say Rice 44
Caster and *By* 45–46
A Universal Language 47
A Universal Language Activity Sheet 48
Symbols 49
Symbols Activity Sheet 50
Egyptian Hieroglyphs 51
Egyptian Hieroglyphs Activity Sheet 52
Codes and Ciphers 53
Sending Secret Messages 54
Deciphering Encoded Messages 55
Solving the Minoan Mystery 56
Masks' Messages 57
Masks' Messages Activity Sheet 58
Nonverbal Communication 59
Nonverbal Communication Activity Sheet 60

Contents
(continued)

Communication Among Animals 61
Talk to the Animals 62
Helen Keller 63
Helen Keller Activity Sheet 64
Labanotation 65
Technological Advances in Communication 66
Technological Advances in Communication Activity Sheet 67
Out-of-This-World Technology 68
Communications as a Career 69
Correlated Activities 70–71
Posttest 72
Answer Key 73
Competent Communicator Award 74

Economics **75–112**
Bulletin Board Ideas 76
Learning Center Ideas 77
Pretest 78
What Is Economics? 79
Economic Headlines, 1776–1976 80–81
Economic Headlines of the Future 82
Barter 83
Money 84
From Goldsmiths to Banks 85
Coins 86
Create a Coin 87
Paper Money 88
Design a Dollar 89
Coming to Terms with Money 90
American Economic Values 91
American Economic Values Activity Sheet 92
Economic Systems 93–94
Economic Systems Activity Sheet 95
Federal Income Tax 96
The Market System 97
The Market System Activity Sheet 98
Competition 99
Competition Activity Sheet 100
Regulations—Good or Bad? 101
Scarcity and Choices 102
Scarcity and Choices Activity Sheet 103
The Potlatch 104
Inflation 105
Depression 106
Urban Economic Problems 107
Innovations and the Economy 108
Correlated Activities 109
Posttest 110
Answer Key 111
Enterprising Economist Award 112

To the Teacher

The activities in this book have been selected especially for gifted students in grades 4 through 8 and are designed to challenge them and to help them develop and apply higher-level thinking skills. These activities have been grouped in the following sections: Advertising, Communication, and Economics.

Advertising

Advertising is calling something—a candidate, an idea, a product, or a service—to the attention of the public, especially by means of paid announcements in print or broadcast media. Approximately $33 billion is spent on advertising in the United States each year. Thus, advertising is a big business that has a big effect on the way millions of Americans think, buy, and live. In this section, students will have an opportunity to explore both the means and the effects of advertising.

Communication

One definition of communication is "a process by which information is exchanged between individuals or groups by means of a shared and mutually understood system of symbols, signs, or behaviors." Thus, communication may be accomplished by means of a long conversation or a fleeting smile, by written and spoken words, or by sounds, gestures, and movements. In this section, students will have an opportunity to study the history of human communication and to become more familiar with its four essential components: the communicator, the recipient, the message, and the medium.

Economics

Economics is the study of how people use their resources to meet their needs and to satisfy their wants, and of how they decide to distribute and consume the goods and services they acquire and produce. Thus, economists focus their attention on the producer, the consumer, the market in which goods and services are sold or exchanged, and any system or philosophy by which that market is influenced or controlled. They use both economic data and economic models to help them understand the past, analyze the present, and predict the future. In this section, students will confront some of the dilemmas faced by economists and become familiar with the workings of the free enterprise system.

In studying these three sections, you may wish to focus on the ways in which they are interrelated. For instance, advertising is one form of communication; and advertising has a direct effect on the economy. If automobile manufacturers were not allowed to advertise their products, what might happen to car sales? How might this affect the jobs of auto workers and steelworkers? What other areas of the economy might be affected and in what ways?

To the Teacher
(continued)

Within each of the three sections are bulletin board and learning center ideas, a pretest and a posttest, as many as thirty activity pages, detailed instructions for more than sixty activities, suggestions for additional correlated activities, an answer key, and an award to be given to students who satisfactorily complete the unit of study. These materials may be used with your entire class, for small-group instruction, or by individual students working independently at their desks or at learning centers. Although you may want to elaborate on the information presented, each activity has been described so that students can do it without additional instruction.

All of the activities within this book are designed to provide experiences and instruction that are qualitatively different and to promote development and use of higher-level thinking skills. For your convenience, these activities have been coded according to Bloom's taxonomy. The symbols used in this coding process are as follows:

KN **knowledge**   recall of specific bits of information; the student absorbs, remembers, recognizes, and responds.

CO **comprehension**   understanding of communicated material without relating it to other material; the student explains, translates, demonstrates, and interprets.

AP **application**   using methods, concepts, principles, and theories in new situations; the student solves novel problems, demonstrates use of knowledge, and constructs.

AN **analysis**   breaking down a communication into its constituent elements; the student discusses, uncovers, lists, and dissects.

SY **synthesis**   putting together constituent elements or parts to form a whole; the student discusses, generalizes, relates, compares, contrasts, and abstracts.

EV **evaluation**   judging the value of materials and methods given purposes; applying standards and criteria, the student judges and disputes.

These symbols have been placed in the left-hand margin beside the corresponding activity description. Usually, you will find only one symbol; however, some activities involve more than one level of thinking or consist of several parts, each involving a different level. In these instances, several symbols have been used.

Advertising

Bulletin Board Ideas

What Makes a Good Television Advertisement?

- ● an intriguing opening
- ● enticing copy
- ● a brief, simple message
- ● essential information
- ● key selling points

Match Game

Match each slogan with the correct company or product. On a piece of lined paper, write the numbers from one through thirteen. Then, beside each number, write a letter from the list below.

1. Get Met. It Pays.
2. Imported from America
3. The Club that beats the streets
4. The ultimate driving machine
5. When it rains, it pours.
6. The right choice
7. Have you driven a _____ lately?
8. Soup is good food.
9. An American Revolution
10. You've got the future on the line.
11. Sharing is caring.
12. The art of engineering
13. Don't leave home without it.

a. American Express Card
b. AT&T
c. Audi
d. BMW
e. Boys Club
f. Campbell's
g. Chevrolet Nova
h. Dodge
i. Ford
j. GTE Sprint
k. Metropolitan Life
l. Morton salt
m. The Salvation Army

Key: 1. k, 2. g, 3. e, 4. d, 5. l, 6. b, 7. i, 8. f, 9. h, 10. j, 11. m, 12. c, 13. a.

Learning Center Ideas

Create a Radio Commercial

1. Choose a product.
2. Create a slogan or jingle for the product.
3. Write a script for a radio commercial in which you use the slogan or jingle to sell the product.
4. Indicate in the script where you will use background music or sound effects.
5. Choose students to be announcers and/or actors.
6. Give them time to get acquainted with the script.
7. Tape record the commercial.
8. Play the commercial for the other members of your class.

Make a Montage

Using advertisements cut from old magazines, make a montage illustrating a general theme or a specific advertising technique. Label it and add it to our display.

Name _____

Pretest

Circle the letter beside the best answer or the most appropriate response.

1. Another name for calling something to the attention of the public, especially by means of paid announcements, is
   a. communicating.
   b. announcing.
   c. propagandizing.
   d. advertising.

2. Because oral language comes before written language, the earliest advertisers were probably
   a. circuses.
   b. shopkeepers.
   c. village criers.
   d. guild members.

3. Long ago, shopkeepers began to put signs above their doors to let passersby know what goods and services were offered within. These signs consisted primarily of simple picture symbols because
   a. many people could not read.
   b. they were cheap to make.
   c. guild members insisted on them.
   d. they were easy to see.

4. In ancient Rome, a **scriptor**
   a. created ads for newspapers.
   b. wrote public notices on walls.
   c. sold writing supplies.
   d. wrote scripts for plays.

5. Soon after Johann Gutenberg devised the process of printing from movable metal type, the emphasis in advertising shifted to
   a. town criers and picture signs.
   b. handbills and posters.
   c. sandwich boards and skywriting.
   d. radio and television.

6. One American printer and publisher devoted more space in his *Pennsylvania Gazette* to advertising than did any other newspaper publisher. What was this publisher's name?
   a. Thomas Jefferson
   b. P. T. Barnum
   c. William Randolph Hearst
   d. Benjamin Franklin

7. The first "soap operas" were
   a. radio programs sponsored by the manufacturers of laundry products.
   b. musical comedies about housewives and housework.
   c. daytime television programs.
   d. musical jingles that helped consumers remember brand names.

8. During the 1950s, television became a major advertising medium. Today, if you watch television for one hour, about how many commercial messages will you see?
   a. four
   b. eight
   c. fifteen
   d. twenty-five

9. **Propaganda** is
   a. a form of advertising.
   b. facts, information, or ideas that are deliberately spread.
   c. intended to help one cause or to hurt another.
   d. all of the above.

10. In which country is the most money spent on advertising?
    a. the United States
    b. England
    c. Canada
    d. Japan

What Is Advertising?

Advertising is calling something—a candidate, an idea, a product, or a service—to the attention of the public, especially by means of paid announcements in print or broadcast media. Most of the advertisements you see and hear are in newspapers and magazines or on radio and television. Businesses advertise their products and services, nonprofit organizations like the Boy Scouts and Little League advertise their programs, and special interest groups advertise their ideas. During election years, political parties spend millions of dollars to advertise their candidates. More than forty-eight thousand advertising agencies help these businesses, groups, and individuals get their messages across to their intended audiences.

Many people believe that advertising plays a very important role in supporting economic growth. Approximately $33 billion is spent on advertising in the United States each year. This figure represents about $155 per person. Printing and broadcasting are expensive processes. Both print and broadcast media rely on advertising dollars to meet their expenses. Without advertising, many newspapers and magazines would go out of business, and many radio and television stations could not exist. For example, in the United States, the country in which more money is spent on advertising than in any other country, there are more than five thousand radio and television stations. Countries with little or no advertising have only one or two stations. In addition, the United States Postal Service earns about $2½ billion each year from the postage on advertisements sent through the mail. Truly, advertising is big business!

Activity

KN Some advertising analysts claim that the average person is bombarded with sixteen hundred advertising messages each day. On one day, keep track of all of the advertising messages that you hear and see, including those in newspapers and magazines; those on radio, television, billboards, and theater marquees; and those in more unusual places, such as on the sides of balloons or all across the sky. What is your total?

Early Advertisements

"Hot-cross buns! Get your hot-cross buns!" The village criers who shouted this message were among the first advertisers. They were chosen for their pleasant and convincing voices just as radio and television announcers are chosen today. Criers announced the arrival of ships at ports along the Nile, described goods for sale in Babylonian markets, and called attention to the slaves, animals, and other wares available in Greek cities.

Later, tradesmen and shop owners hung signs over their doors to show what goods and services they had for sale. Most signs were pictures because few people could read. As more and more people learned to read and write, written advertising became more common. The Romans created a wall divided into white-washed rectangles on which a *scriptor*, or writer, wrote in charcoal. Sales, services, and festivals were advertised on this wall. Announcements praising the qualities of gladiators have been found on the ancient walls of Pompeii.

The invention of the printing press gave advertising a big boost. Suddenly, it was possible for shopkeepers to print up hundreds of handbills or posters to advertise their wares. In 1480, the first known advertisement printed in England announced the sale of a book. Advertisements soon began to appear in newspapers. The first newspaper advertisement offered medicine for sale. During the seventeenth century, newspaper advertising became common, and public notices similar to today's classified ads were carried in most newspapers. By the eighteenth century, English newspapers were being financed by advertising.

Name _____

Early Advertisements Activity Sheet

KN
CO
AP
1. The English word **circus** comes from the Latin word *circus*, meaning "a circular line, a ring, or an oval racecourse." In ancient Rome, the *circus* was not a show but an arena. It was a round or elliptical structure with tiers of seats that enclosed an open space. Within this space were held races, games, and gladiatorial combats. The most famous ancient *circus* was the Circus Maximus in Rome. Originally built in the sixth century B.C. and later rebuilt by Julius Caesar, this circus seated 350,000 people and was the site of chariot races and other spectacles. Pretend that you are a Roman *scriptor,* or writer. It is your job to write an advertisement for an upcoming event at the Circus Maximus. First, find out more about this remarkable arena. Then, on a separate sheet of paper, create an advertisement that will convince your fellow Romans to attend the event.

KN
CO
AP
2. The modern circus, which dates from the late eighteenth century, is a traveling show that features animals, acrobats, and clowns who perform in rings. Advance advertising for circuses is often done by means of posters. On a separate sheet of paper, create a poster for a modern circus, carnival, or fair. Include the name of the event, the dates on which it will take place, and the prices that will be charged for admission. Don't forget to describe the "special attractions" that might appeal to the members of your audience and make them more eager to attend.

KN
CO
AP
3. In Western Europe during the Middle Ages, persons who were in the same business or shared the same craft joined together in groups called **guilds.** The primary purposes of these groups were to provide protection and status for members, to establish conditions for labor, and to set standards for workmanship and price for products. In a time when relatively few persons could read, many of the guilds adopted pictorial symbols for their crafts and trades. These symbols were used on ornate signs hung over shop doors to identify the types of products or services that were for sale within. Design a medieval pictorial sign that could be used to identify one of the following modern businesses: a computer store, a sporting goods store, a television station, or a travel agency.

Name _____

Advertising in America

Advertising came to America with the colonists. The first paid advertisements in this country, which were circulated in 1704, offered rewards for the return of lost or stolen merchandise.

Benjamin Franklin played an important role in the development of newspaper advertising in America. A printer and publisher, he devoted more space in his *Pennsylvania Gazette* to advertising than did any other newspaper publisher. Franklin advertised books, lumber, tea, ships' sailings, and his own invention—the Franklin stove. To improve the appearance of his ads, he used headlines and small illustrations, and arranged them so that they were less crowded than those run by his competitors.

Another early form of advertising was **billposting**, a method in which printed advertisements were attached to signboards or walls. The earliest bills and posters consisted of a few words, often announcing a theater performance or public event. Later, artwork was added. During the nineteenth century, American showman P. T. Barnum used billposting to advertise his circus, and collectors still value the posters on which he immodestly announced upcoming performances of "the Greatest Show on Earth."

The availability of a free public education in the United States helped to develop a large reading audience, and the approval of special low postal rates for certain types of printed matter gave advertisers inexpensive access to this audience. Mailboxes were soon stuffed with brochures, catalogs, fliers, letters, and offers of all sorts.

The first commercial radio station, WWJ in Detroit, Michigan, began regular broadcasts on August 20, 1920. A little more than one year later, the federal government issued the first license to broadcast regularly to station WBZ in Springfield, Massachusetts. Within seven years, there were five hundred licensed stations, and radio had become an important medium for advertising. Colgate, Palmolive, and Proctor and Gamble advertised soaps, shampoos, and laundry products on programs that came to be known as "soap operas," and musical jingles helped listeners remember brand names and recall product benefits.

Name _____

Advertising in America
(continued)

Television was developed during the 1920s but did not begin to play an important role in mass communication until the late 1940s. During the fifties, 70 percent of radio's audience switched to television, and so did its advertisers. As recently as 1982, such large companies as Bristol-Myers, Chrysler, Coca-Cola, Colgate-Palmolive, General Foods, General Mills, Gillette, Johnson and Johnson, Kellogg, Nabisco, PepsiCo, Pillsbury, Proctor and Gamble, and Ralston Purina were spending more than three-fourths of their advertising dollars on television commercials.

Activities

AN 1. Analyze the direct-mail advertising that your family receives to determine what types of products are most often advertised in this way. Save all of the advertisements that come to your house by mail for an entire month. Sort them into piles according to the type of product that is being advertised in each piece. Create a chart or graph to illustrate the results of your analysis.

AN SY 2. Radio soap operas got this name because they were sponsored by companies that manufactured shampoos, soaps, and laundry products. Watch a television soap opera to discover which companies sponsor these programs today and what types of products are advertised. Then speculate about the probable composition of the regular viewing audience for this show and about whether or not these products would appeal to members of this audience.

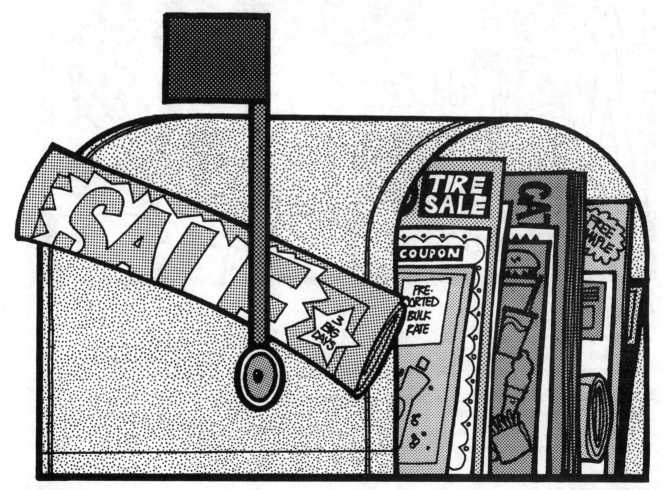

Name _____

Outdoor Advertising

Outdoor advertising takes many forms, from playbills to skywriting; but the most popular form is billboards. Nearly one-half million billboards advertising everything from cruises to cold remedies line America's streets and highways. They are placed where they will be seen by thousands of passing motorists and pedestrians each day.

A billboard display usually consists of a large, eye-catching picture with a brief message. The message must be brief because the average passerby sees it for only a few seconds. Billboard displays are created by pasting sheets of printed paper side by side on a signboard. Their purpose is twofold: to introduce consumers to new products and to remind them of familiar ones.

Outdoor advertising can create problems. For example, in cities signs may be safety hazards if they divert the attention of pedestrians and motorists from the flow of traffic. Along highways, billboards may detract from the scenic beauty of the countryside. For these reasons, the governing bodies in many cities and counties have passed ordinances regulating the size, density, and location of outdoor signs and billboards.

Activities

KN CO 1. Do some research to learn about the limitations placed on outdoor advertising by the city or county in which you live. What sizes of signs are permitted and under what conditions? Where are billboards allowed? How many may be used? How far apart must they be placed?

AP 2. Many people object to billboards along highways because they clutter the landscape and hide more attractive natural scenery. Think about this problem. Then, devise a form of outdoor advertising that is more in harmony with the surrounding environment. Explain your ideas by means of drawings and labeled diagrams.

Name _____

Futuristic Outdoor Ads

AP During the next one hundred years, outdoor advertising will change drastically. First, think of a method of outdoor advertising that might appeal to buyers in the future. Then, use this method to advertise a product that might be manufactured in the future. Sketch a picture of your product and ad ideas in the space below. As you do so, remember that a good outdoor advertisement should be eye-catching and that the message should be brief.

Name _____

Magazine Advertising

Until the advent of television, magazines were the largest national advertising medium. Many advertisers recognized there were several advantages to advertising in magazines rather than in newspapers. For example, because magazines were published weekly or monthly rather than daily, deadlines were longer, and more care could be given to the design, layout, and typography used on magazine pages. Also, because magazines were printed on white paper with a slick finish, elaborate color ads could be reproduced in this medium. Magazines were created to appeal to specific groups of people who shared a common interest such as careers, cars, decorating, gardening, home-making, news, politics, or sports, advertisers could select and target the appropriate market or audience for the product or message they were trying to promote.

When television began to take advertising dollars away from magazines, magazine advertising and promotion departments answered the challenge by becoming more creative. For example, in 1957, a new advertising technique was used to sell a well-known brand of coconut flakes in a major national magazine. The ad was printed in an ink perfumed to smell like coconut oil. Since that time perfumed inks and "scratch-and-sniff" techniques have been used to promote a variety of scented products, including air fresheners, cosmetics, perfumes, and soaps.

Activities

KN CO AN
1. Select several magazines that would appeal to groups of people with very different interests. Choose several specific types of products, such as laundry soaps, makeup, shaving preparations, and automobiles. Count the number of times each one of these products is advertised in each magazine. Use a line or bar graph to illustrate the results of your magazine advertising survey.

AN SY
2. Select one magazine designed to appeal primarily to women in the home and another designed to appeal to women in the business or professional world. Compare the advertisements in these two magazines. In what ways are they similar? In what ways are they different? In words or pictures, create a composite that represents the feminine ideal suggested by the ads, articles, and illustrations on the pages of each magazine.

Name _____

Techniques Used in Magazine Advertisements

The purpose of most advertisements is to persuade consumers to buy specific products. To achieve this goal, advertisers use a variety of persuasive techniques. For example, they emphasize the strong points or unique features of a product. They describe the care with which a product is designed and manufactured and list its ingredients or safety features. They call attention to the present image or long-standing reputation of the company that makes the product. Or they suggest the reliability of the product by mentioning the terms and provisions of the warranty.

Advertisers also use special appeals to sell their products. For example, they appeal to the consumer's desire for status by creating the impression that no life is complete without a particular car, suit, or watch. Or they appeal to the consumer's penchant for hero worship by having a show business personality or sports celebrity endorse a product, thereby suggesting that it will make its users happier, healthier, or more attractive.

In addition, magazine advertisers use headlines to attract reader attention, logos to help readers associate products with brand names, and slogans to help consumers remember product benefits and features.

AP AN Analyze some magazine advertisements to see what persuasive techniques are used in them. Record what you learn in the table below.

Company or Brand	Product	Persuasive Technique

Television Commercials

If you watch television for one hour, you will see about fifteen commercial messages. Although television commercials have the same purpose as magazine or newspaper ads, they differ from these ad forms in one very important way. They cannot be read again and again. To be effective, the message presented in a television commercial must be understood and remembered from a single viewing.

The main goal for the writers and artists who produce television commercials is to quickly make a lasting impression. To do so, they use famous people or memorable characters like clowns, green giants, or animated figures. Sometimes, they add catchy tunes and clever slogans to create what they hope will be an indelible memory of the product they are trying to sell.

Television offers both advantages and disadvantages to advertisers. Television commercials are expensive to produce, but they reach millions of people at one time. Also, by carefully selecting the time of day, type of program, or part of the country in which commercials will be shown, advertisers can direct their messages to the audiences that are most likely to buy their products. For example, advertisements for children's toys would probably yield better results if shown on a Saturday morning rather than on a weekday morning, and the market for ski equipment is probably greater in the Rocky Mountain states than in Hawaii!

Activities

KN
CO 1. From advertisements in old magazines, cut pictures of unusual characters designed to catch your
AP   attention. Use these pictures to make a montage.

AN 2. Explain why the use of unusual characters in advertisements is widespread and comment on
EV   whether or not you believe it is effective.

AN
SY 3. List all of the advertising slogans you can remember. Compare your list with the lists created by
EV   friends or classmates. In what ways are they similar? In what ways are they different? Specifically,
       what qualities make slogans easy for *you* to remember? In general, what qualities make slogans
       easy to remember?

Name _____

Hookers and Grabbers

What do you do when the television program you are watching is interrupted by a commercial message? Many viewers hurry to the kitchen for a snack, make a telephone call, or talk to the family members or friends with whom they are watching the program. Advertisers know viewers will ignore commercial messages that do not interest them. For this reason, they encourage copywriters to "grab," or forcefully engage the attention of, viewers during the first seven seconds of a commercial, before they have time to look or move away from the screen.

The device copywriters use to capture and hold the attention of viewers is called a **grabber** or a **hooker.** It is an action or statement so funny, startling, or intriguing that viewers are fascinated and are forced by it to pay attention to the commercial message that follows. In other words, they have been **grabbed** and are **hooked,** at least for the next thirty seconds or so.

The grabber, or hooker, gets the viewers' attention; but the commercial message, itself, convinces them to buy the product. This message should be simple and not obscured by all sorts of irrelevant or useless information. It should be brief but enticing and should include a few key selling points. These points should be clearly stated and then repeated so that consumers will remember them when making a purchase or confronted with a product choice.

Activities

AN 1. Producing a commercial is expensive. For this reason, many advertisers do not make separate commercials for radio and television. Instead, they produce a commercial for television and then use it on radio. List the ways in which a commercial made exclusively for radio might differ from one made for use on radio and television or from one made exclusively for television.

AN SY EV 2. First, listen to a commercial on radio and make a few notes about your impressions of it and your reactions to it. Next, view the same commercial on television and, again, make some notes regarding your impressions and reactions. Finally, compare your reactions to the two commercials. In which medium is this commercial more convincing? Why?

AP AN SY EV 3. If you were hired to rewrite and reproduce this commercial exclusively for use on radio, what specific changes would you make so that it would be more effective in this nonvisual medium?

Name _____

Identifying Types of Television Commercials

KN
CO
AP

Television commercials are created by a team of people that includes writers, artists, producers, directors, film and sound crews, set designers, casting agents, and actors and actresses. The specific type of commercial they create depends on the kind of product they want to sell and on the method they believe will sell it most effectively.

On this page and the one that follows are descriptions of seven familiar types of television commercials. First, read each description carefully. Then, on the line provided, write the name of one or more products that have been sold using this type of commerical.

Celebrity Endorsements—In commercials of this type, a celebrity comes on the screen and talks about a product. Because viewers are inclined to take the word of a celebrity at face value, the Federal Communications Commission has ruled that statements made on television by famous people must be true and that the proof must be furnished upon request.

_____

Hidden Camera Techniques, Interviews, and Testimonials—Commercials of this type feature people who have used the product and who tell you how wonderful it is. Sometimes, the people in these commercials are actual users of the product. Other times, they are actors who have been hired to play the role of consumer, or product user.

_____

Major Musical Productions—Commercials of this type are often used to sell soft drinks and fast food. They feature relatively large casts whose members sing and dance their way through fancy sets. Their purpose is to entertain as well as to sell.

_____

Identifying Types of Television Commercials
(continued)

Real Life Drama—Although fictional, these playlets give the appearance of having captured a slice of life and are frequently used to sell products for the home.

_____

Special Effects Commercials—Commercials of this type use animation, computer graphics, special filters, and slow motion, stop motion, and time lapse photography to create artificially the effects of the past, the future, space, another world, or elapsed time. They are often used to sell automobiles, computers, and other devices associated with high technology and high performance.

_____

Table Top Commercials—As the name suggests, commercials of this type were first used to sell food displayed on counter or table tops. In the past, advertisers frequently used plastic food or unrealistic setups in these commercials; but the Federal Trade Commission ruled that the product being displayed on television must be the one being advertised in the commercial. Today, no substitutes are permitted.

_____

Unique Viewpoint Commercials—Commercials of this type are made from up high, down low, or underwater. They create a dramatic effect by showing the product from an unusual angle, side, or perspective.

_____

Propaganda

Many people are automatically suspicious of anything that is called "propaganda." This word is often used to label the information-spreading activities of dishonest persons or totalitarian governments. But propaganda is not necessarily misleading and need not have anything to do with politics. In fact, the English word **propaganda** comes from the Latin phrase *congregatio de propaganda fida,* which means "congregation for propagating the faith" and was the name given to an organization formed by Pope Gregory XV to spread the doctrine of the Roman Catholic Church throughout the world. Since Gregory's time, many churches have used propaganda to attract new members.

Propaganda is a form of advertising. It is facts, information, or ideas that are deliberately spread to help one cause or to hurt another. Thus, when a manufacturer mails out pamphlets to persuade consumers to buy a particular beauty preparation or laundry product, he is spreading propaganda.

Companies that manufacture products are not the only publishers of propaganda. Both totalitarian governments and democracies use propaganda to create, shape, and control public opinion. The primary difference is that, in a dictatorship, citizens may be forbidden to express or publish ideas that differ from the official government position. In a democracy, the free exchange of ideas is encouraged, and the rights of the citizens to free speech and a free press are protected. Thus, in a democracy, writers and speakers may safely express their own ideas even if they disagree with the government; however, they may be held responsible for the truthfulness of their facts and the consequences of their actions.

How does propaganda work? Effective propaganda is usually written in words that are "loaded," that is, have strong connotations and tend to arouse powerful emotions, such as love, hate, or fear, or appeal to the need of people to be respected and to feel superior. Thus, propaganda may warn of a threatened invasion, inform parents that a child without a computer is doomed to fall hopelessly behind his classmates, or caution women that time is taking its toll on their skin. In each of these instances, it is the intent of the propagandist that those who read or hear these messages fear invasion and hate the invader; love their children, want them to be superior, and buy them computers; or hate and fear the wrinkles of age and be willing to buy some expensive cream to prevent or erase them.

Activities

AN SY 1. During World War II, both the Allies and the Axis Powers used propaganda to promote their points of view. If possible, read and compare some of the speeches delivered by Winston Churchill, Adolf Hitler, and/or Franklin Roosevelt. In what ways are they similar? In what ways are they different? What is the primary purpose of propaganda during wartime? In what ways was this purpose achieved in the speeches you read?

SY 2. During a war, all possible media and means are used to rally public opinion in support of the war effort. For example, during World War II, not only did radio commercials urge people to buy war bonds, support the Red Cross, and grow victory gardens, but also popular songs and motion pictures aroused patriotic feelings and encouraged dislike and distrust of the enemy. Watch part of a movie made during World War II. Notice the way in which the Germans or Japanese are portrayed. While the primary purpose of this movie was to entertain, it had another purpose as well. What was this secondary purpose?

Name _____

Subliminal Advertising

The process of advertising has long been a subject of controversy. The purpose of advertising is usually to persuade someone to support a candidate, buy a product, or use a service. Many critics argue that advertisers often go too far in their efforts to persuade and actually convince people to make decisions against their will so that they buy products they do not need and pay for services they cannot afford. As one frightening example, these critics cite subliminal advertising.

The word **subliminal** means "outside the area of conscious awareness." Thus, **subliminal advertising** is commercial messages that viewers are not aware they are seeing or have seen. Subliminal advertising was the brainchild of a public relations executive named James Vicary. In 1956, he held a press conference in which he described this technique as being so powerful that no one could resist it and so subtle that no one would realize what had happened. In theory, the advertisers who used subliminal advertising would be able to change the opinions and buying patterns of the public at will.

To prove his point, Vicary cited the results of an experiment he had conducted in a local movie theater. During the feature, the phrases "Drink Coke" and "Eat Popcorn" were flashed on the screen. They appeared and disappeared so quickly that people in the audience were not really aware of them, yet theater employees working in the lobby refreshment stand reported that Coca-Cola sales increased by 57 percent and popcorn sales, by 18 percent. Vicary claimed that people in the audience purchased Coca-Cola and popcorn because their unconscious minds told them to do so in terms so strong that their conscious minds could not resist. The news media immediately condemned James Vicary for having foisted a new form of mind and behavior control on a gullible and unwilling world.

Actually, there is no scientific proof that hidden messages affect what people do or buy. One possible explanation for the results Vicary obtained is that the moviegoers had intended to buy refreshments from the moment they entered the theater and were simply "reminded" by these "subliminal" messages to do so. Other possible explanations are that the weather was unusually warm or that some other factor, of which Vicary was not aware and for which he did not control, caused the notable increase in soft drink sales. In the more than thirty years since Vicary's press conference, there has never been a well-controlled scientific study demonstrating that subliminal advertising works.

Activity

SY
EV
Many critics say that advertising—whether subliminal or not—can be used to manipulate people, that is, to skillfully control their thoughts and actions. What do you think? Is advertising manipulative? If so, under what circumstances? Is this manipulation dangerous? If so, in what ways? Should advertising be controlled? If so, by whom and in what ways?

Advertising Regulations

How often have you seen an advertisement that has been either misleading or offensive to you? Most people who work in the advertising business are aware of their responsibility not to prepare, produce, or print false or deceptive advertisements. They realize that deceptive advertising causes buyers to be disappointed and may result in physical or economic injury.

For this reason, in 1962, the American Association of Advertising Agencies published a code in which its members promised not to publish advertisements that contain false or misleading statements or pictures offensive to public decency, and not to distort price claims, scientific statements, or testimonials.

Unfortunately, while many advertisers could agree to sign the code, they could not agree on definitions of the terms **deceptive** and **offensive.** As a result, the Federal Trade Commission (FTC) and the courts have had to establish rules regarding deception. These agencies realize that the purpose of advertising is to persuade and that most ads are biased toward the product

they are trying to persuade consumers to buy. For this reason, FTC rules permit a practice known as trade puffing. **Trade puffing** is exaggerating the features, qualities, or benefits of a product by claiming that it is "the best" or "the greatest." The FTC also permits the use of fantasy characters—green giants, elves, talking animals, or animated cartoon characters—because its members believe that viewers readily classify these characters as fictitious and are not deceived by them.

If products do not meet the standards claimed for them in advertisements, the FTC may find the advertisements misleading and the advertiser guilty of deception. If so, the advertiser must run corrective ads to eliminate any misconceptions the false ads may have caused. In one instance, a company was charged with running television commercials that showed children riding bicycles in an unsafe manner. In response to urging by the FTC, the company agreed to make a bike safety announcement that was run on television as a public service message.

Activities

AN 1. The FTC is concerned that celebrity endorsements of products may be misleading. List five to ten guidelines you would suggest to ensure that advertisements of this type would not be deceptive.

AN SY 2. Some critics have suggested imposing a regulation that would limit television commercials to showing the products, themselves, and would prohibit the use of live models and attractive or dramatic backgrounds. List some of the advantages and disadvantages of such a regulation.

Correlated Activities

KN
CO Cut out different types of magazine advertisements and arrange them on a bulletin board. Label these ads according to the specific advertising techniques used in them.

CO
AP Some marketing programs are designed to persuade people to change their behavior. For example, advertising campaigns have been developed to encourage people to stop smoking, to avoid littering, and to refrain from driving while under the influence of alcohol or drugs. First, collect examples of some of these kinds of advertisements. Then, develop your own public service ad for a cause you think is important.

AP Create a newspaper ad, magazine ad, or radio commercial for one of the following products: a fast-food product, a miracle shampoo, a toothpaste especially for children, or a trouble-free camera.

CO
AN The *Saturday Evening Post* became a huge success as a magazine; however, in 1968, it went out of business because it could not attract enough advertisers or subscribers. Yet in that same year, about one hundred new magazines appeared on the market! Take a survey to determine which magazines are read regularly by the members of your family or class. Share the results of your survey by means of a line or bar graph.

CO
AN Observe body language in advertisements. Notice eye talk, hand gestures, and head position. How does body language affect your feelings about the product that is being advertised? Which is more important, what a television announcer says or what he does?

AP
AN
SY Pretend that you are the advertising manager for a large department store. You have been asked by the president of the store to determine the effectiveness of the store's current advertising campaign. What methods will you use and what will you learn from each one of them?

Make mine a Monsterburger!

Correlated Activities
(continued)

CO Investigate the costs of running ads of various sizes in a variety of publications. For example, you might consider newspapers, telephone directories, programs printed for high school or college athletic events, and yearbooks. Share what you learn by means of a chart, table, or graph.

AN SY Compare the rates you obtained in the activity above. What factors might account for the differences among them? Consider, for example, circulation, permanence, and potential for reaching the intended audience or market.

AP Create a humorous ad for one or more of the following fairy-tale products: a nonscary spider for Little Miss Muffet, a horn for Little Boy Blue, apples for Snow White, shampoo for Rapunzel, or a construction business specializing in single-family dwellings run by the Three Little Pigs.

AN Surveys show that the television viewing audience differs widely, depending on the time of day and the type of program. For this reason, companies choose to advertise certain types of products during certain types of shows. For each type of show named below, list two products that could be advertised successfully: cartoon special, cooking show, evening news special, football game, and spy mission.

AN Not long ago, it was considered unprofessional for a doctor or dentist to advertise her or his services or fees. Members of these groups were allowed to list only their name, telephone number, office location, and specialty or nature of practice in the telephone directory. Describe some of the advantages and disadvantages of medical advertising.

SY Media critics voice concern about the possible relationship between television violence and street violence. They suggest that seeing violence makes us calloused to it so that we become more willing to condone it and more able to commit it. As an advertiser, what standards would you set for the programs you sponsor? Explain your answer.

SY EV **Bloopers** are embarrassing public blunders. Because television commercials are filmed, the bloopers that occur in them can be edited out before they are shown. Usually, it is not possible for people to rerun their lives and undo the mistakes they have made; but if it were possible, what "bloopers" would you edit out of the past week?

Answer Key

Pretest, Page 10		Posttest, Page 29	
1. d	6. d	1. d	6. d
2. c	7. a	2. a	7. d
3. a	8. c	3. b	8. a
4. b	9. d	4. c	9. c
5. b	10. a	5. b	10. b

Name _____

Posttest

Circle the letter beside the best answer or the most appropriate response.

1. **Advertising** is
   a. calling something to the attention of the public.
   b. usually biased.
   c. important to the U.S. economy.
   d. all of the above.

2. During the seventeenth century, newspaper advertising became common. Today, without advertising, many newspapers would
   a. go out of business.
   b. have more editorial freedom.
   c. have more space for news articles.
   d. hire more reporters.

3. A form of advertising that was popular in early America was
   a. skywriting.
   b. billposting.
   c. radio commercials.
   d. bumper stickers.

4. Within seven years after the first commercial radio station began regular broadcasts, radio had become an important advertising medium. In which decade did this development take place?
   a. 1900–1910
   b. 1910–1920
   c. 1920–1930
   d. 1930–1940

5. During the fifties, when television began to take advertising dollars away from magazines, magazine advertising executives countered by
   a. boycotting television.
   b. becoming more creative.
   c. offering free ads.
   d. regulating television commercials.

6. As recently as 1982, such large companies as Coca-Cola, General Foods, Nabisco, PepsiCo, and Pillsbury were spending what fraction of their advertising budget on television commercials?
   a. less than one-fourth
   b. exactly one-half
   c. almost two-thirds
   d. more than three-fourths

7. To attract reader attention, magazine advertisers use
   a. animated figures and catchy tunes.
   b. hidden camera techniques and major musical productions.
   c. sound effects and special effects.
   d. headlines, logos, and slogans.

8. Today, the most common form of outdoor advertising is
   a. billboards.
   b. skywriting.
   c. neon signs.
   d. banners.

9. **Subliminal advertising** is
   a. subtle but powerful.
   b. effective but illegal.
   c. commercial messages viewers are not aware they have seen.
   d. the most popular form of advertising in the world today.

10. What government agency has the primary responsibility for regulating advertising practices in the United States?
    a. Food and Drug Administration
    b. Federal Trade Commission
    c. Interstate Commerce Commission
    d. American Association of Advertising Agencies

This is to certify that

_____

(name of student)

has satisfactorily completed a unit of study

on

Advertising

and has been chosen as an award winning

Advertising Executive

in recognition of this accomplishment.

_____

(signature of teacher)

_____

(date)

Communication

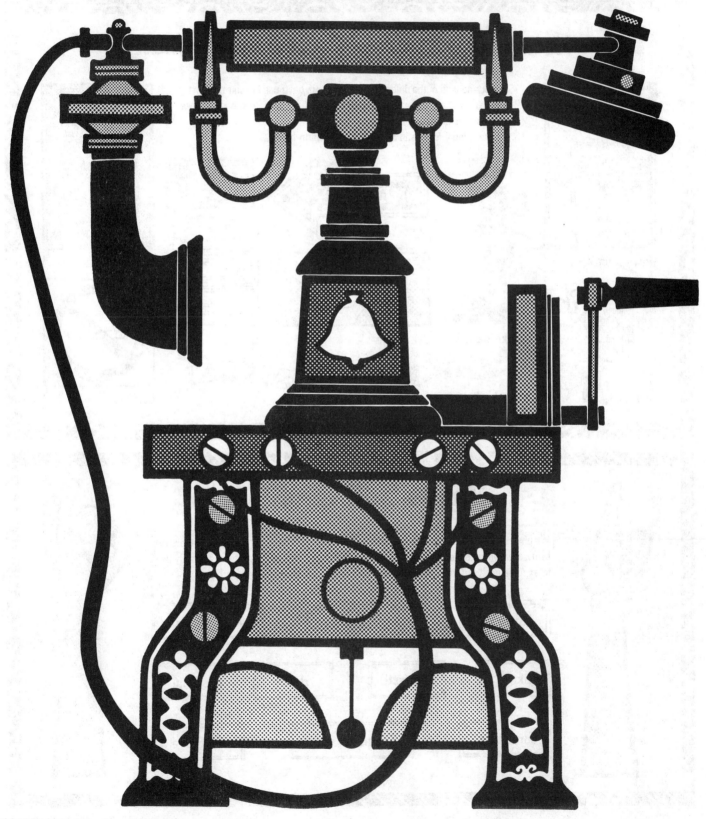

Bulletin Board Ideas

Communication—Past and Present

1. Think about all of the different means people have used to communicate.
2. Find and cut out an example or draw a picture of at least one of these means of communication.
3. Create a label for it and add it to this bulletin board.

newspapers

smoke signals

signs

drawings

letters

posters

symbols

drums

sky banners

Hands Tell the Story

We often use hand movements, or gestures, to communicate. Each of the ideas expressed below in words can also be expressed nonverbally, by hand. What gesture is usually used to express each of these ideas? What other ideas can be expressed by hand?

Hurry up!	Victory	It stinks!
Okay.	Perfect!	Hello!	Stop!
Come here.	Shame on you!	Good-bye.

Learning Center Ideas

Make a Mask

1. Use the materials at this center to create your own mask.
2. Write a play or choreograph a dance in which you can wear your mask.

Classroom Correspondence Center

Use the supplies at this center to write a letter. Address it to a family member, friend, classmate, teacher, elected official, community group, or newspaper editor.

The Wonderful World of Writing

CUNEIFORM   GREEK ALPHABET   CHINESE CHARACTERS   EGYPTIAN HIEROGLYPHICS   MAYA GLYPHS

1. Choose a writing system that interests you.
2. Investigate to learn when and by whom it was developed, the number of characters on which it is based, and how long it has been or was in use.
3. Use this system to write a message.
4. Compare this system with the writing system you usually use. In what ways are they similar? In what ways are they different? Which system do you prefer? Why?

Name _____

Pretest

Circle the letter of the best answer or the most appropriate response.

1. Around 3100 B.C., the ancient Egyptians developed a complex writing system in which they used small pictures that stood for words or ideas. These pictures are called
   a. pasigraphs.
   b. photographs.
   c. cryptographs.
   d. hieroglyphs.

2. In A.D. 105, in response to orders from the Chinese emperor, Ts'ai Lun found a way to make paper from
   a. a tufted marsh plant.
   b. animal hides.
   c. the inner bark of the mulberry tree.
   d. threads from a caterpillar's cocoon.

3. During the Middle Ages, European monks laboriously
   a. carved stone monuments.
   b. copied books by hand.
   c. published newspapers.
   d. erected pyramids.

4. Around A.D. 1450, Johann Gutenberg invented the process of printing
   a. from wooden or clay blocks.
   b. by means of a rotary press.
   c. on parchment or papyrus.
   d. from movable metal type.

5. In 1876, Alexander Graham Bell invented
   a. the phonograph.
   b. the telegraph.
   c. television.
   d. the telephone.

6. A **bilingual** helps linguists translate messages written in unknown scripts. A bilingual is
   a. a word that is the same in two languages.
   b. a document on which the same message is written in two languages.
   c. a picture that has two linguistic interpretations.
   d. a language that is spoken in two countries.

7. A **cryptographer** analyzes
   a. crystals and minerals.
   b. codes and ciphers.
   c. handwriting.
   d. ancient tombs.

8. A **cartouche** is
   a. an oval or oblong figure enclosing the name of an Egyptian ruler.
   b. an English place-name that exhibits Latin linguistic influence.
   c. a sedge, or tufted marsh plant.
   d. a printing block made of clay.

9. **Esperanto** is
   a. a special form of American sign language.
   b. the last name of the English architect who deciphered Linear B.
   c. a simplified regular language developed by Lazarus Ludwig Zamenhof.
   d. an Eskimo word for snow.

10. Basically, communication is a form of sharing that involves
    a. talking.
    b. listening.
    c. understanding.
    d. all of the above.

Name _____

Communication Time Line

20,000 B.C. Prehistoric people recorded their thoughts and observations in pictures painted on cave walls.

3500 B.C. The Sumerians developed a type of pictographic writing that later evolved into **cuneiform.**

3100 B.C. The Egyptians discovered how to make a material on which they could write from a tufted marsh plant called **papyrus** and began to develop a complex writing system based on picture symbols called **hieroglyphs.**

2100 B.C. The earliest known library, a collection of clay tablets, was established in Babylonia.

540 B.C. The first public library was built in Athens, Greece.

200 B.C. During this century, the Romans began to post written copies of official announcements in public places.

100 B.C. Some copyright laws, censorship, and a system of public libraries existed in the Roman world.

59 B.C. *Acta Diurna* (Daily Events), the earliest known newssheet, was started in Rome, Italy. This publication, which was publicly posted rather than privately distributed, was, nonetheless, a forerunner of the modern newspaper.

A.D. 105 Ts'ai Lun of China perfected a method of making paper.

A.D. 400–1400 European monks laboriously copied and illuminated manuscripts by hand.

A.D. 700 The world's first printed newspaper, a Chinese circular called *Ti-pao,* was printed during this century from carved wooden blocks.

A.D. 1034 In China, Pi Sheng invented movable type made of baked clay.

A.D. 1450 In Mainz, Germany, Johann Gutenberg perfected the process of printing from movable metal type. Several years later, Gutenberg used his process to print an edition of the Bible.

A.D. 1564 Shepherds in Borrowdale, England, found the purest graphite yet discovered and used it to brand their sheep.

A.D. 1609 *Avisa Relation oder Zeitung,* the first regularly published newspaper in Europe, was started in Germany.

A.D. 1622 Nathaniel Butter published the *Weekly News,* the first English publication that resembled a modern newspaper.

A.D. 1653 A public library was opened in Boston, Massachusetts.

A.D. 1690 Benjamin Harris of Boston, Massachusetts, published the first newspaper in colonial America, which was called *Publick Occurrences Both Forreign and Domestick.*

A.D. 1702 The *Daily Courant,* the first daily newspaper in England, was published.

A.D. 1790–1795 French chemist Nicholas Jacques Conté mixed pulverized graphite with clay and baked this mixture to produce a writing material that could be marketed in strips.

A.D. 1790s French engineers Claude and Ignace Urbain Chappe invented an extensively used telegraph system that employed visual signals.

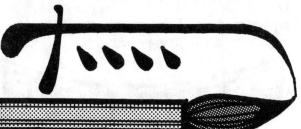

Communication Time Line
(continued)

1791 The first ten amendments to the U.S. Constitution were ratified by three-fourths of the states. The first of these amendments guaranteed United States citizens freedom of religion, of speech, and of the press and granted to those citizens the rights to assemble peaceably and to petition the government for a redress of grievances.

1799 A large stone bearing a message from an Egyptian king was found near Rosetta, Egypt. Because the message was written in both Greek letters and Egyptian hieroglyphs, this stone enabled French Egyptologist Jean François Champollion to equate the unfamiliar hieroglyphs with familiar Greek words and, thus, to decipher Egyptian hieroglyphics.

1822 French physicist Joseph Nicéphore Niepce made the first photograph, a **heliograph** or **heliotype** produced on a glass plate coated with bitumen.

1839 Louis Jacques Mandé Daguerre, a scene painter for the opera, announced that he had successfully used mercury vapor to obtain permanent pictures on coated metal plates.

1844 The Chappe telegraph network connected twenty-nine French cities through five hundred stations.

1850 The first international telegraph cable was laid between Calais, France, and Dover, England.

1858 The first transatlantic telegraph cable was laid between Ireland and Newfoundland.

1870 A compulsory education law passed in England marked the beginning of official governmental efforts to eliminate illiteracy.

1872 Motion-picture pioneer Eadweard Muybridge was hired by Leland Stanford to prove that a race horse had all four feet off the ground at one time during its running gait. Muybridge devoted himself to photographing animals in motion and invented the **zoopraxiscope**, by which he reproduced moving pictures on a screen.

1876 Alexander Graham Bell invented the telephone.

1877 Thomas Alva Edison invented the phonograph.

1879 George Eastman patented a machine to coat glass photoplates with liquefied, light-sensitive gelatin.

1884 Eastman invented a machine that would turn a roll of paper into photographic film.

1893 Edison developed the **kinetiscope**, a forerunner of the motion picture projector, and later demonstrated experimentally the synchronization of moving pictures and sound.

1895 After developing wireless telegraphy, Italian physicist Guglielmo Marconi transmitted communication signals through the air as electromagnetic, or radio, waves over a distance of more than one mile.

1901 Marconi received in St. John's, Newfoundland, the first transatlantic wireless signals, sent from his station at Poldhu, Cornwall, England.

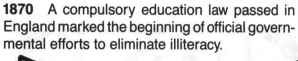

Name _____

Communication Time Line
(continued)

1903 President Theodore Roosevelt sent a telegram around the world. His message took nine minutes to travel approximately 24,000 miles.

1921 The U.S. government issued the first license to broadcast regularly to radio station WBZ in Springfield, Masschusetts, on September 15.

1929 Vladimir K. Zworykin demonstrated the first practical television system.

1941 Regularly scheduled television programs were broadcast from the Empire State building.

1948 The first tape recorder was manufactured in the United States.

1957 Sputnik, the earth's first artificial satellite, was launched by the U.S.S.R. on October 4.

1959 American astronomers established radar contact with Venus.

1960 The first lasers were manufactured in the United States. The Xerox Corporation perfected a photocopying process known as xerography. Echo I, the first communications satellite, was launched.

1962 Another communications satellite, Telstar I, began relaying telephone conversations and television programs between the United States and Europe.

1966 The first home video game units were introduced.

1970s Microprocessors were developed. Cassette videotape recorders were introduced.

1972 Pong, the first popular video game, was marketed.

1975 The first personal computer, the Altair 8800, was produced and sold in kit form.

1976 Steve Wozniak and Steve Jobs created the forerunner of the Apple computer in their garage.

1978 The computer game Space Invaders was introduced in Japan and grossed more than $600 million in one year.

1980s Videodiscs, compact discs, and projection and large-screen television sets were marketed.

Activities

CO
AP
AN

1. Some of the events listed in the time line are not technological in nature, yet they have had a profound effect on the history and development of communication. For example, the ratification of the first amendment to the U.S. Constitution in 1791 has had a tremendous impact on newspaper and other forms of publishing in the United States. Select one nontechical event that has been important in the development of communication. Explain its importance and analyze its impact.

AN
SY
EV

2. You are doing a feature story on the five most important communication advances in human history. Look at those listed in the time line and think about others of which you are aware. Choose five and explain in detail why you have chosen each one.

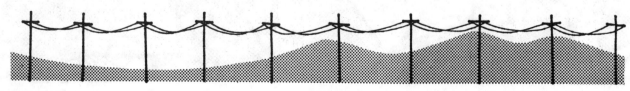

Name _____

What Is Communication?

The English word **communication** is closely related to the Latin noun *communicatio*, which means "a sharing," and to the Latin verb *communico, communicare*, which means "to share something with others." One definition of communication is "a process by which information is exchanged between individuals or groups by means of a mutually understood system of symbols, signs, or actions." But communication is more than the exchange of information. It is a pleasant conversation with a good friend, a night at the theater, a television program, a road sign, or a wall of graffiti. It may be accomplished by means of a lengthy discussion or a brief smile, by written or spoken words, or by sounds, movements, and gestures. Communication is all of the ways in which we share facts, fears, feelings, frustrations, ideas, opinions, and dreams.

Communication is a complex process with a long and intricate history. Many observers agree that three changes have drastically affected the history of human communication. The first of these changes took place thousands of years ago when humans first developed a written language. Writing enabled people to keep permanent records and eliminated the need to rely on human memory. The next important change occurred during the fifteenth century when Johann Gutenberg invented the process of printing from movable metal type. Gutenberg's invention transformed printing from a tedious handcraft to a machine process and made possible the mass production of printed pages. Finally, the third change began in the nineteenth century with the work of Thomas Alva Edison, Guglielmo Marconi, Alexander Graham Bell, and others, and is still continuing today. It includes the invention and perfection of numerous technological devices, such as the radio, telephone, phonograph, and telegraph, that have improved the means of communication and made the process faster and more efficient.

Name _____

Communication Diagram

KN
CO
AP

Communication consists of four equally important parts: the message, the communicator, the recipient, and the medium. The **message** is the facts, fears, feelings, frustrations, ideas, opinions, or dreams that are shared, exchanged, or sent. The **communicator** is the person or group who sends the message. The **recipient** is the person or group who receives the message. The **medium** is the means by which the message is sent. The medium may be verbal or nonverbal, spoken or written, print or electronic. The medium may be tone or gesture, conversation or personal letter, newspapers or television.

Complete the communication diagram below by writing a message, name, or description on each numbered line.

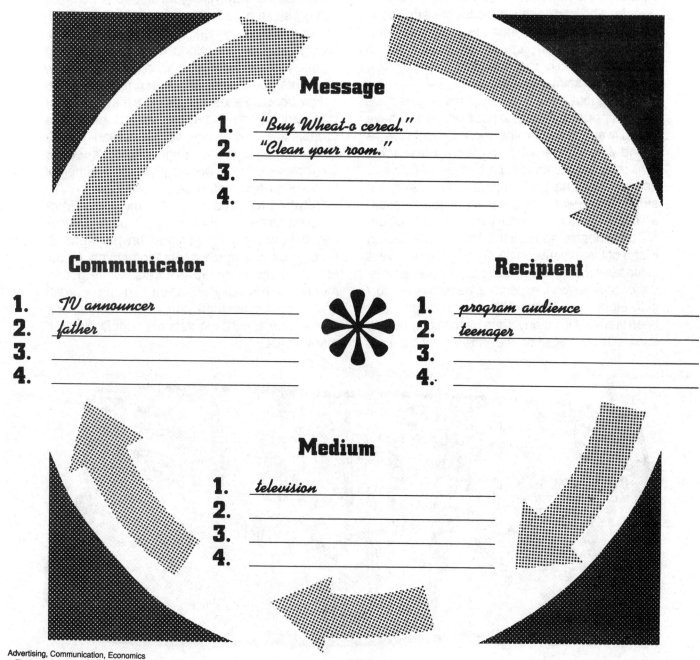

Message

1. *"Buy Wheat-o cereal."*
2. *"Clean your room."*
3. _____
4. _____

Communicator

1. *TV announcer*
2. *father*
3. _____
4. _____

Recipient

1. *program audience*
2. *teenager*
3. _____
4. _____

Medium

1. *television*
2. _____
3. _____
4. _____

From Stone to Paper

Occasionally, when it is necessary to leave a message, writing paper and a pencil or a pen are not readily available. What do you do in this situation? Early scouts arranged sticks or rocks to create trail signs for the travelers coming after them. Some people have scrawled their messages in the dust on table tops or traced them in the moisture that has condensed on bathroom mirrors. Others have used sticks or rocks to scratch important words in dirt or stone. Ancient people, who had neither pencils nor paper, used what was available to them. For example, Cro-Magnons painted pictures on cave walls in southern France, and American Indians drew symbols on animal hides.

Throughout human history, if messages have been important enough to pass on, people have found ways of recording them. The Maya, a Stone Age people who created a remarkable civilization in Mesoamerica between 2000 B.C. and A.D. 900, painted on pottery and carved in stone. Stone was both durable and readily available, but it was hard to carry from place to place.

The Minoans, who inhabited the Mediterranean island of Crete between 3000 and 1400 B.C., kept extensive lists of palace supplies on clay tablets. Clay was relatively inexpensive, easier to transport than stone, and remarkably durable after it had been fired. In fact, many of the Minoan clay tablets survived the ravages of time and weather because a palace fire hardened them to stone. The most famous writings on clay are on the tablets that were part of the earliest known library, established in Babylonia in 2100 B.C. These tablets contain historical information, economic records, scientific treatises, and literary texts.

Around 3200 B.C., the Egyptians discovered how to make a material on which they could write from a tufted marsh plant called papyrus. At the same time, they developed a complex writing system based on approximately seven hundred picture symbols, or hieroglyphs. Painstakingly, Egyptian scribes used reed brushes dipped in ink to write letters, copy reports, keep accounts, log taxes, and make mathematical calculations on sheets of papyrus that were later rolled and stored as scrolls. Papyrus was not as durable as stone or clay; but it was readily available, and it was lighter weight and better suited for a more refined writing style than either of these other two materials.

Between A.D. 400 and 1400, monks in European monasteries laboriously copied and illuminated manuscripts by hand on parchment. Parchment was made by treating animal hides, usually those of sheep or goats. While parchment could be easily written on with pen or brush and was tougher than papyrus, it took a long time to make, and an adequate supply required many hides.

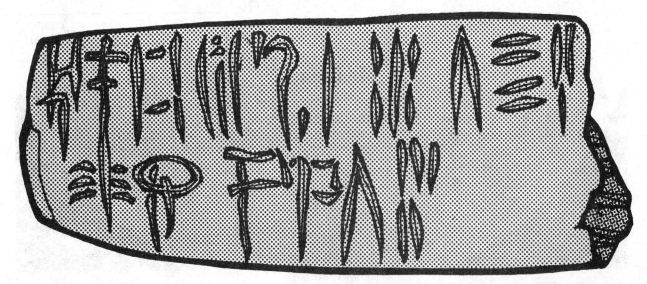

Name _____

From Stone to Paper
(continued)

Through the ages, people have written on many materials—stone, clay, leather, papyrus, and parchment—but none has proved to be as practical as that invented by Ts'ai Lun in A.D.105. In that year, the Chinese emperor ordered Ts'ai Lun to create a new writing material. He took fibers from the inner bark of the mulberry tree, beat them to a pulp, and then pressed and matted them into a sheet. The result was paper, which has proved to be less expensive, more convenient, and more versatile than any other writing surface yet tried. Today, for example, there are more than seven thousand different kinds of paper, each one especially suited to a particular job or use. Not only is paper used for writing, but it is also used for wiping and wrapping as well.

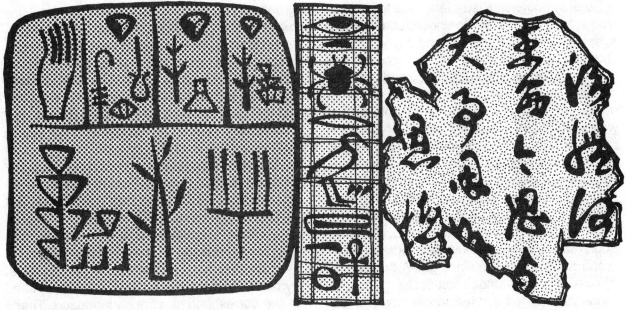

Activities

KN CO
1. First, find out how paper is made. Then, create a chart on which you describe and illustrate the steps in this ancient process.

KN CO AN
2. Have you ever written in glue and then sprinkled it with glitter or scratched with a stick in the sand at a beach? Make a simple chart on which you write and illustrate or provide examples of some of the unusual writing methods and materials you have used. Share your chart with the class.

AP AN
3. Think about the problem posed in the first paragraph on page 40. What would you do if you had an important message to leave and had neither writing paper nor pencil or pen? In a well-known mystery story, the author describes how a blind woman, sensing that she was about to be murdered, used the point of her knitting needle to write the name of her unsuspecting assailant in braille on her desk blotter. In what imaginative ways might you record important information or leave an urgent message?

AP AN SY EV
4. Experiment with different writing materials or surfaces. Try rocks, clay, bark, leather or parchment, and paper. Likewise, experiment with different writing implements. Try rocks, sticks, charcoal, chalk, brush and ink, pen and ink, calligraphic pen, ballpoint pen, and pencil. Which implements worked best on each type of writing surface? Which surfaces and implements were easiest to use? Which combination of surface and implement enabled you to leave the clearest record? The most lasting record? Why?

The Evolution of Language

Language is one of the ways in which people communicate with one another. An **oral**, or **spoken**, **language** is a group of sounds and a system for combining these sounds so that they name objects and express ideas. A **written language** is a system of visual symbols that represent objects, ideas, or sounds. These visual symbols may be simple shapes, elaborate pictures, or alphabet letters.

Before people can use a language to communicate, they must learn to understand it and to speak it. Can you remember the day you spoke your first word? Probably not. Chances are that you were between the ages of nine and eighteen months. Your first word was probably *mama* or *dada*; but before long you were able to say words like *baby, ball, bird, book, brush, bye-bye, car, cat, comb, cookie, dog, feet, hands, ice cream, nose, toes,* and *water.* Your early vocabulary consisted mostly of nouns—words that named things that were important to you. Gradually, you learned adjectives like *bad, cold, good,* and *hot* and verbs like *eat, go,* and *play.* Soon you were putting nouns and verbs together in short sentences like *Baby go.* With practice, you could create longer sentences to ask for things you wanted and tell people how you felt.

As you grew older, you learned to write the letters of the alphabet, to use these letters to spell words, to combine these words to create sentences, to use sentences to construct paragraphs, and finally, to string paragraphs together in letters, essays, and stories.

Many linguists believe that primitive people developed language in much the same way that you learned it. First, they used simple sounds to name objects, make requests, and issue warnings. Gradually, they linked sounds together to express more complex ideas and observations about the world around them. At some point, they needed or wanted to record rather than remember. In response to this need, they began to use visual symbols to write their ideas. Some groups of people used **pictographs**, simple pictures of familiar objects like *bear, fire,* or *mountain.* Other groups of people used **ideograms**, more abstract pictures or pictures that represented more complex ideas. With each of these methods, pictures stood for things or ideas but not for sounds, words, or phrases. Thus, a new picture was needed for each new idea; and a written language of this type might consist of hundreds or even thousands of characters. For example, the hieroglyphic writing system developed between 3100 and 2600 B.C. by the ancient Egyptians contained more than seven hundred characters; and Chinese writing offers more than forty thousand character combinations.

In another type of written language, visual symbols represent the sounds or syllables used in the corresponding spoken language. These symbols are called phonograms. English is a language of this type. Only twenty-six letters are needed to write the English language. These letters can be combined to represent all of the sounds that are used in spoken English and to spell all of the words that are used in written English.

The Evolution of Language Activity Sheet

AN
SY
1. If your parents kept a baby book for you, look in it to discover the age at which you began to talk. Make a list of your first words. Compare your list with similar lists prepared by other members of the class. In what ways are the lists similar? In what ways are they different? On the basis of these lists, what generalizations can you make about the way in which young children learn language?

AN
SY
2. If your parents did not keep a baby book for you, arrange to talk with a family member, a friend, or a neighbor who has a young child. During your conversation, ask when the child learned to talk and what his or her first words were. Make a list of these words. Compare your list with similar lists prepared by other members of the class. In what ways are the lists similar? In what ways are they different? On the basis of these lists, what generalizations can you make about the way in which a young child learns a language?

KN
CO
CO
AP
3. Calligraphers have identified more than forty thousand character combinations in Chinese writing, yet all of these characters are created from only six basic strokes: the horizontal stroke, the vertical stroke, the sweeping left stroke, the sweeping right stroke, the hook, and the dot. Using a felt-tipped pen or a narrow paintbrush dipped in India ink, practice these strokes on a separate sheet of paper.

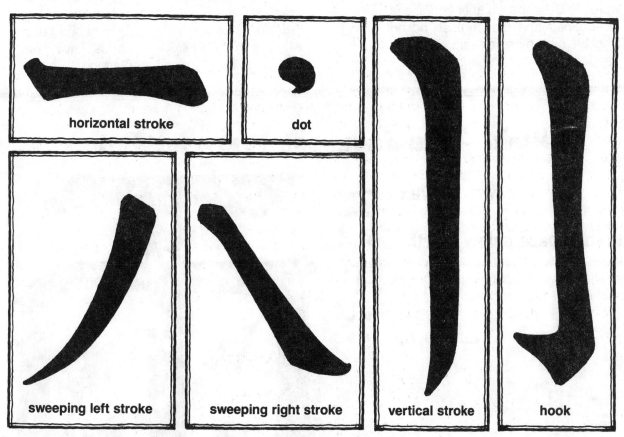

horizontal stroke

dot

sweeping left stroke

sweeping right stroke

vertical stroke

hook

AN
SY
EV
4. The English word **calligraphy** comes from two Greek words meaning "beautiful writing." Calligraphy is an elegant form of handwriting developed and used by monks who painstakingly copied manuscripts by hand during the Middle Ages. If you are familiar with calligraphy, compare the basic strokes used in it with those used in Chinese writing. In what ways are they similar? In what ways are they different? Which writing system would you prefer to learn? Why?

Ninety-Two Ways to Say Rice

Every language—English, Finnish, Korean, and nearly three thousand others—is a product of the people who speak it and a reflection of the culture in which it was developed. Languages usually begin as a few words. These words enable their users to name their basic needs for food, clothing, and shelter and to express their feelings of fear, joy, love, and pain. New words are added as the need arises; and in this way, the language grows. Gradually, specialized collections of words and phrases, or vocabularies, are developed to express complex ideas about the arts, religion, science, and social life.

Most linguists believe that geography and climate have a profound effect on language development. For example, in English there are many words to describe weather conditions, but most dictionaries and thesauruses do not offer an English synonym for rain. English-speaking people differentiate among fog, mist, rain, snow, sleet, and hail; but not among kinds of rain. To them, rain is rain. They are very matter-of-fact about weather.

The story is very different in Japan. People living in that vulnerable island nation have learned to welcome and appreciate gentle rain to protect themselves from the devastating downpours that characterize Pacific storms. Japanese dictionaries and thesauruses list as many as seventy-five different words associated with rain. Among these words are *ame* (rain), *amaashi* (falling rain), *akisame* (autumn rain), *harusame* (spring rain), and *amadare* (raindrops from house eaves).

There are many other examples of the close association between language and culture. For example, one Eskimo group has twelve separate words for snow. And the Hunanóo people, who live in the Philippine Islands, have ninety-two words for rice, their staple food.

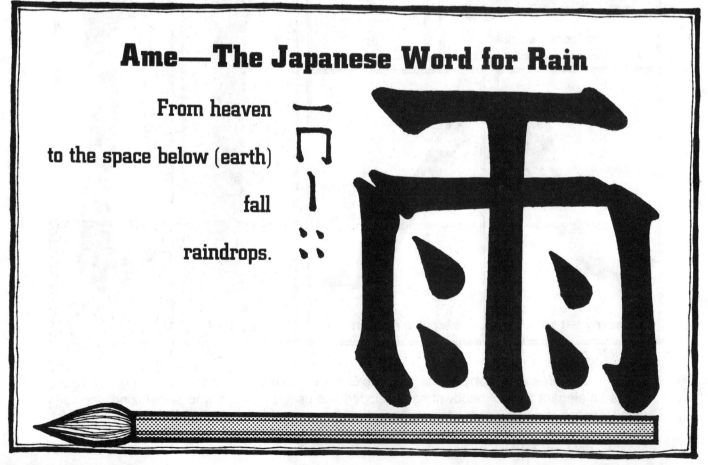

Ame—The Japanese Word for Rain

From heaven

to the space below (earth)

fall

raindrops.

Caster and *By*

Languages seldom develop entirely in isolation. When groups of people trade and fight with one another, their languages are often indelibly affected by their intermingling. Words are borrowed from older languages for use in new ones, and conquering countries leave their linguistic marks on the languages spoken in the territories they occupy.

The English we speak, which linguists call Modern or Standard English, came from Middle English, which, in turn, came from Old English. Old English was the language spoken in England between A.D. 450 and 1140. It was, at first, a combination of the dialects brought to English shores by the Angles, the Saxons, and the Jutes. During its first seven hundred years, Old English came into contact with the languages spoken by the Celts, the Romans, and the Scandinavians and was permanently influenced by them.

Between 200 B.C. and A.D. 200, the Romans conquered most of the known world, extending their empire from Syria and Armenia in the east to Britain in the west. Because Roman troops lived and fought in these places, Latin—the language they spoke—influenced the languages spoken throughout this vast area. For example, the Latin word *castrum* (pl. *castra*), meaning "stronghold, fortified camp, or encampment," became the Old English word *ceaster.* In English, the meaning of this word was generalized so that it was used to designate any enclosed place intended for habitation, including ancient walled towns and medieval castles. Today, English place-names such as Dorchester, Manchester, Winchester, and Lancaster still reflect this Latin linguistic influence.

The Scandinavian influence on English was perpetuated by trade and conquest. Between A.D. 787 and 1050, Scandinavian sailors from what are now Denmark and Norway periodically invaded and permanently settled in Britain. As a result, Danish and Norse became the usual languages spoken in some parts of that country, and Norse was still spoken in Scotland as late as the seventeenth century. Such English words as *dike, egg, get, give, gold,* and *kid* are of Scandinavian origin. The Danish word *by* means "farm or town." Thus, evidence of Danish influence can be seen in such English place-names as Derby, Rugby, and Thoresby and in the word *by-law,* which originally meant "town law."

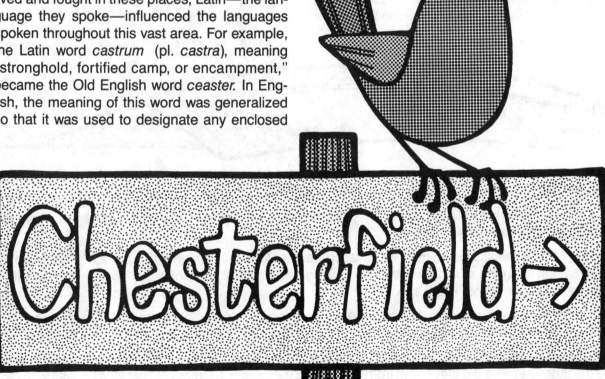

Caster and *By*
(continued)

When Old English and Scandinavian were mingled, there were many instances in which each language had a word for a particular idea or concept. In some instances, as English developed, the Old English word was retained. In other instances, the Scandinavian word came to be used in place of the Old English equivalent, which was discarded. And in still other instances, Scandinavian and Old English words continued to coexist so that the language contained both. Below are listed examples of Old English and Scandinavian words that are a part of Modern English and are synonyms.

Old English	Scandinavian
craft	skill
from	fro
hide	skin
no	nay
rear	raise
sick	ill
whole	hale

Altogether, about nine hundred words that exist in Standard English today are Scandinavian in origin.

Activities

KN **1.** On a map of Great Britain, find place-names that show Latin and Scandinavian influence. Make an alphabetical list of these names.

CO AP AN **2.** Look at the specific locations of these place-names. Are they clustered in a particular geographic area—in the north or in the south, along the coast or inland? If you observe some sort of pattern, what factor or factors might account for it?

KN CO **3.** Do some research to learn when the Romans invaded Britain, who their military leader was, how long they stayed, and why they left.

KN CO **4.** Do some research to find the answers to these questions: Who were the Angles, the Saxons, and the Jutes? Where did they come from? When did they settle in Britain? What kind of language did they speak? Where did the name *England* come from?

Name _____

A Universal Language

Thousands of different languages and dialects are spoken in the world. More than one hundred and fifty languages are found in India alone. Because linguistic differences are barriers to effective communication and often lead to serious misunderstandings, linguists have long dreamed of creating a single, universal language that could be learned, spoken, and understood by all people in all nations throughout the world.

In 1887, Polish linguist Lazarus Ludwig Zamenhof developed a language that he hoped would become the world's universal language. He thought his language would make it possible for ambassadors, businessmen, and tourists to communicate easily and effectively with people who spoke languages other than their own and would promote international understanding and world peace.

Zamenhof published his work under the name of Doktoro Esperanto, which means "Doctor Hopeful." **Esperanto**, as his language came to be called, is a simplified, regular language with Latin-type grammar and a European vocabulary. More than one million people around the world speak and read it. Newspapers, journals, and literary works have been published in this language. In addition, Esperanto is the official language of several radio stations that broadcast programs around the world.

Although Esperanto is popular in some parts of the world, it still has not become the universal language Zamenhof and other linguists dreamed of creating. Some scientists believe that the only truly universal language will be a computer language. They speculate that the widespread use of computers will lead to the creation of an artificial, culturally unbiased tongue—one that even beings from outside the solar system will be able to understand.

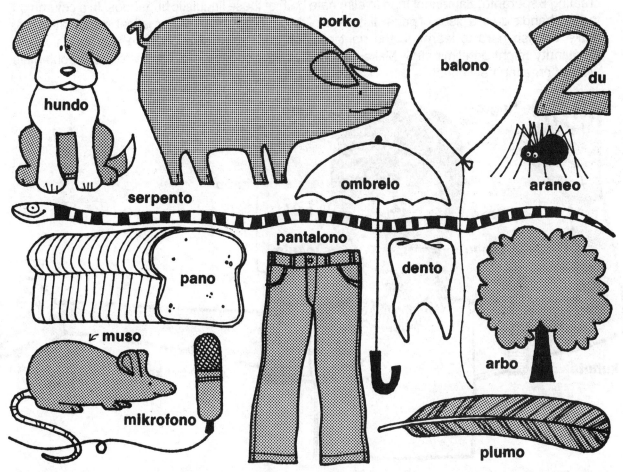

A Universal Language Activity Sheet

KN
CO

1. People who speak the same language may occasionally have trouble understanding one another because some of their terminology is different. For example, although English is spoken in both England and the United States, different words are used in each place for some common items. In England, gasoline is called *petrol* (short for *petroleum*), and a baby carriage is called a *perambulator.* Talk with someone who has lived in England or read a portion of a book or article written by an English author to discover other instances in which the English and Americans have different names for the same thing. List all of the examples you are able to find. Compare your list with the lists created by other members of your class. Were they able to find some examples you missed?

KN
CO
SY

2. The last paragraph of the article on page 47 speaks of the eventual creation of an artificial language that is "culturally unbiased." What do the words **culturally unbiased** mean? Offer several examples to show that English, or any other language with which you are familiar, is culturally biased.

KN
CO

3. Do some research to learn more about Esperanto. Where is it spoken? What efforts have been and are being made to encourage its adoption? What does written Esperanto look like? What does spoken Esperanto sound like? If possible, find and photocopy a passage written in Esperanto and share it with the class.

KN
CO
AP

4. Perhaps you have learned a spelling or grammar rule, used the rule to spell a word or answer a question on a test, and then lost points because the situation named in the question was "the exception that proves the rule." Irregularities and exceptions make a language difficult to learn. In creating Esperanto, Zamenhof tried to eliminate both of these linguistic bugaboos. In a column on the left-hand side of a piece of paper, list some of the spelling and/or grammatical irregularities that make English hard to learn. To the right of each one, suggest a sensible way in which the irregularity might be eliminated. Make certain that your suggestions eliminate old irregularities *without* creating new ones!

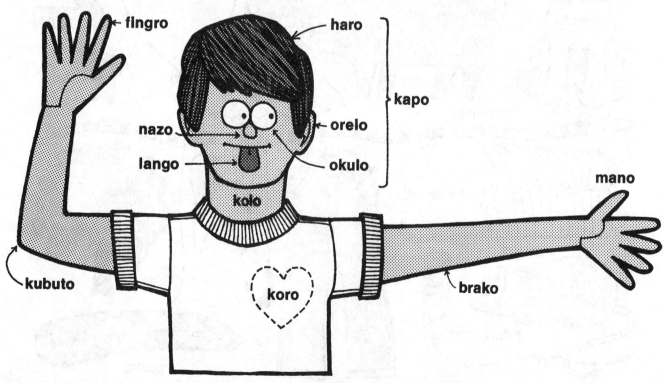

Symbols

Some psychologists believe that the one quality which sets humans apart from other creatures and makes them unique among the inhabitants of the earth is their ability to symbol, to create sounds and pictures that represent feelings and ideas. It is this ability that has made it possible for humans to develop complex oral and written languages and to alter developed language systems to fit new situations and to express new ideas.

A **symbol** is an object, person, place, or event that can be used to stand for, represent, or suggest something else because of traditional association, emotional content, or accidental resemblance. For example, an apple may be used in some contexts to suggest school because of traditional association. For the same reason, a four-leaf clover symbolizes good luck.

Symbols can be classified as visible or audible, depending on whether they are designed primarily to be seen or to be heard. The apple and clover are visible symbols, but a siren is an audible symbol of distress. Its wail warns of approaching danger.

Recently, organizations concerned with travel have been instrumental in creating **pasigraphy**, an artificial, international written language based on pictures rather than on words. Pasigraphic signs in airports, train stations, and other public places enable travelers to identify the men's and women's restrooms, to locate the baggage claim area, to find a coffee shop or restaurant, and to obtain first aid or information easily, even though they cannot read or speak the language of the country in which they are visiting.

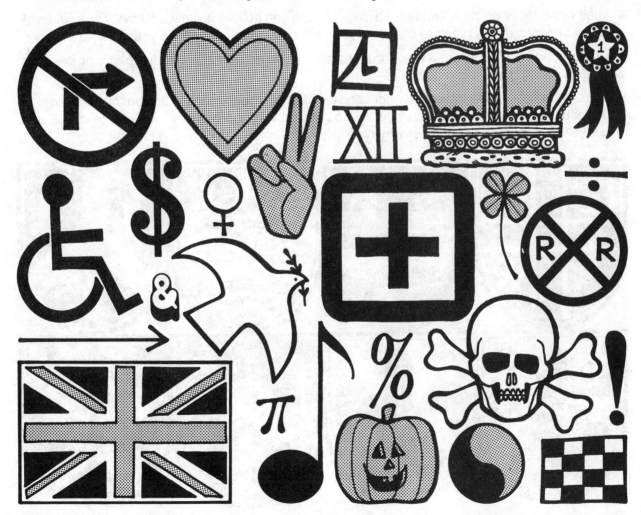

Symbols Activity Sheet

KN
CO
1. During the 1800s, cattle were allowed to graze freely in the American West on unfenced land called open range. Each rancher developed a simple symbol to mark his calves so that cowboys tending the herd would be able to tell which animals belonged to which spread. Do some research to learn more about cattle brands. Share what you learn with the class by means of a chart on which you picture some famous brands, name the ranch for which each one stood, and tell something about the ranch itself. For example, you may wish to tell where it was located, how big it was, who owned it, and how long it was in operation.

CO
AP
AN
2. A **logogram** is a letter, symbol, or sign used to represent an entire word. A **logotype** is a single group of words or a block of type that is used as an advertising symbol. Logos are not a creation of modern society. In fact, they have been in use for thousands of years. Each pharaoh of ancient Egypt was represented by a **cartouche**, and each important family of the Middle Ages had a **coat of arms** . First, do some research to learn more about the symbolism associated with cartouches and coats of arms. Then, on a piece of paper or tagboard, create a cartouche, coat of arms, or modern logo for your family. Be prepared to explain its symbolism to the class.

KN
CO
3. Many businesses have logograms and/or logotypes. Businesses with logos often use them on their stationery and in their advertisements. Create a montage of logos cut from newspaper and magazine advertisements.

SY
EV
4. Look at the logos on your montage. Choose the one you believe is most effective. On a separate sheet of paper, draw an enlarged picture of it and explain the reasons for your choice.

AP
5. Create a name and design a logo for a business engaged in manufacturing paper or ink, or in printing, binding, or selling books.

AN
SY
EV
6. Look at the name and symbol that appear on the copyright page (page 2) and on the back cover of this book. What do they make you think of? Do they make a good logo for a publisher of educational books for young people? Why or why not?

Egyptian Hieroglyphs

The ancient Egyptians valued records. To one of their gods they entrusted the painstaking task of weighing souls and keeping accounts. Around 3100 B.C., they discovered how to make a writing material from papyrus, a tufted marsh plant that grew in abundance in the fertile Nile Valley. They also devised a system of symbols that enabled them to record thoughts and events.

At first, the Egyptian system of writing was fairly simple. It was based on the use of **hiero-glyphs**, or small pictures that stood for words or ideas. As this writing system evolved, the hieroglyphs came to represent sounds. Still later, the Egyptians put these sound-representing hieroglyphs together to form words very much as we do with letters of the alphabet. There is, however, one major difference between the modern English alphabet and the ancient Egyptian system of hieroglyphs: in the English alphabet, there are twenty-six letters; in the ancient Egyptian system of hieroglyhs, there were more than seven hundred characters.

Because the ancient Egyptian writing system was so complicated, only a few people mastered it. For the most part, these people were the **scribes**. The English word **scribe** comes from the Latin noun *scriba*, which means "official writer" and is related to the Latin verb *scribere*, meaning "to write." Egyptian scribes were educated men, trained to read, write, and perform certain mathematical calculations and administrative tasks. These men were both respected and powerful. In fact, a well-trained and ambitious scribe might win appointment to any position he chose—priest of a temple, governor of a province, or advisor to the pharaoh.

For centuries, modern scholars remained puzzled by the extraordinary form of writing developed and used by ancient Egyptian scribes. Then in A.D. 1799, a broken slab of basalt unearthed near Rosetta, Egypt, provided the clue they needed. Carved in its surface was a message from an Egyptian king. Because this message had been composed when the Greeks ruled Egypt, it was written in both Greek letters and Egyptian hieroglyphs. At first, scholars were still unable to understand how the Egyptian message corresponded to the Greek one. Then, in 1822, a French Egyptologist named Jean François Champollion discovered a way to recognize the names of ancient Egyptian rulers, which appeared on the stone in both Egyptian hieroglyphs and Greek letters. This discovery enabled Champollion to equate the unfamiliar hieroglyphs with familiar Greek words and, thus, to unlock the secret of the hieroglyphic message.

Egyptian Hieroglyphs Activity Sheet

KN CO 1. In ancient Egypt, there were no typewriters, printing presses, or photocopiers. Personal and governmental documents and correspondence had to be written or copied by hand. This tedious task was performed by scribes. Scribes carried kits with all of the necessary writing implements. In fact, such a kit was found in Tutankhamon's tomb. Find a picture or description of one of these ancient scribe's kits. List or draw and label pictures of its contents.

KN CO 2. Think about the number of English words you know that are related to the Latin verb **scribere**, meaning "to write." For example, there are **scribble, scribe, script, scriptorium, inscribe, inscription, prescribe,** and **prescription.** First, list all of the words you can think of on a sheet of paper. Then, look up and write the meanings of these words beside them.

KN CO 3. **Papyrus** is a sedge, or tufted marsh plant. It was so universally used in ancient Egypt that it became the hieroglyphic symbol for Lower Egypt and was a common motif in Egyptian art. Do some research to discover some of the many ways in which the Egyptians used papyrus. Then share this information with your class by means of a poster or chart.

CO 4. Discover and describe in detail how papyrus was made into writing material, or a kind of paper.

AP 5. What is a **cartouche**? First, look up the meaning of this word. Then, discover what use Champollion made of cartouches. Finally, design your own hieroglyphic designation and place it inside a cartouche.

AP 6. In some ways, a message written in hieroglyphs resembles a rebus. Both are combinations of pictures that stand for ideas and of symbols that stand for sounds, syllables, or words. Create a rebus about a person or event that was important in the history of communication.

Name _____

Codes and Ciphers

Almost everyone is fascinated by secret messages. Children sometimes exchange coded notes and hope that parents and teachers will not intercept and decipher their messages, and the hapless victim can be rescued in the nick of time if the fictional spy is able to crack the code and read the cryptic message written on the matchbook that was surreptitiously slipped to him.

A **code** is a system of symbols—letters, numbers, pictures, or words—that are assigned special meanings and are used to communicate messages. **Cipher** is one kind of code. It is a method of systematically changing a written text to conceal its meaning by substituting new letters for existing ones.

When you want to send a message in code, you must devise a code, and then you must put your words into code or cipher form. You must **encode** or **encipher,** your message. If you receive a message written in a code with which you are familiar, you must **decode,** or **decipher,** it to figure out what it says. If you receive a message written in a code that is unfamiliar to you, you must **crack,** or **break,** the code before you can begin to decipher the message.

The process of enciphering and deciphering messages written in a secret, or unknown, code is called **cryptography,** and specialists in this field are called **cryptographers.** In times of war or national emergency, their work becomes critically important because accurate understanding of a coded message can make the difference between failure and success for important military missions.

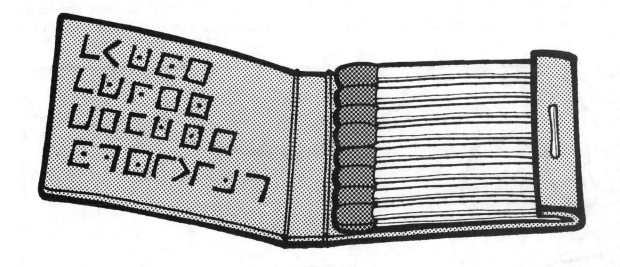

Activity

KN CO During World War II, the language of the Navajo Indians was used by the United States to send secret messages. This language is one of the most difficult languages in the world to learn, and very few people speak it. Do some research to learn more about the Navajo Indians, their language, and its use as a code during the war.

Name _____

Sending Secret Messages

Ciphers and codes have been around since the dawn of recorded history. The Greeks used shorthand ciphers. They devised ingenious ways to encode messages and were very clever at hiding them as well. For example, one wealthy Greek shaved the head of his slave, wrote an encoded message on the man's bald pate, and waited until the hair grew back to send the messenger on his journey. When the message-bearing slave was captured and searched, his captors were unable to discover where the message had been hidden, and they let him pass. In another incident, an important message was hidden in the belly of a dead rabbit. Disguised as a hunter, the messenger was able to carry the rabbit and the message through enemy lines.

The ancient Chinese wrote their secret messages on very thin pieces of paper which they crumpled into tiny balls and coated with wax. In this form, the messages could be easily hidden in the ear or mouth, or even swallowed if necessary.

In the last century B.C., Caesar and Cicero used codes in ancient Rome while Cleopatra was developing her secret ciphers in Egypt.

During the Renaissance, secret messages were frequently sent, and even royalty used codes. When Mary, Queen of Scots, was imprisoned in England, she exchanged letters with Anthony Babington, a conspirator who was trying to assassinate the reigning English monarch, Queen Elizabeth I, and release Mary. Of course, Mary encouraged him. Meanwhile, Francis Walsingham, Elizabeth's secretary of state, had set up an organized and efficient system of secret intelligence to detect plots against the English queen. Unfortunately for Mary, her letters fell into the hands of Walsingham's spies. Even more unfortunately, the code in which Mary had written her letters was all too easily deciphered. Charged with being an accomplice in Babington's plot, Mary was tried and found guilty, largely on the basis of her own letters. On February 8, 1587, she was beheaded.

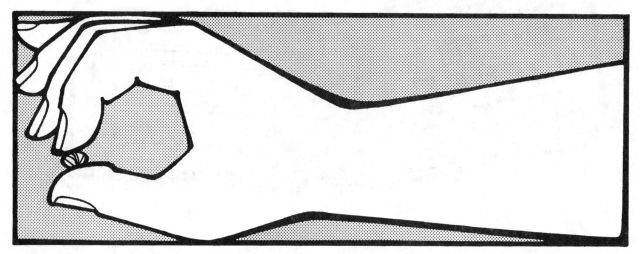

Activities

CO 1. Until the sixteenth century, there was not much need for codes because relatively few people could read or write. Writing, itself, was a kind of "code," because few people could understand written messages. Do some research to discover the ways in which people sent messages *before* they could read or write. Share what you learn with the class by means of a chart or poster.

AP 2. Use one of the communication methods you read about in activity 1 to send a message to a friend.
AN
SY Then evaluate your results. How successful were you at sending the message? How successful was your friend at receiving and understanding the message? Did he or she get only the general idea or understand *exactly* what you had said?

Name _____

Deciphering Encoded Messages

Before there were computers to help decipher encoded messages, cryptographers spent weeks, months, and even years trying to crack a single code. Among the clues they used were the frequency of individual letters and the patterns made by letter combinations. For example, the letter *E* is the most frequently used letter in the English language. It appears in more than half of all words and 126 times in every 1,000 letters.

The next most common letters are *T, O, A,* and *N.* After *T* and *N,* the letters *R, D,* and *S* are the most frequently used consonants. *N* is the consonant that most often follows a vowel. *T* is the consonant most commonly used to begin a word, and *E* is the letter most often found at the end of a word. The consonants *D* and *N* are also frequently used to end words.

The only one-letter words in the English language are *A* and *I.* The most frequently used two-letter words are prepositions—*in, of,* and *to. The* and *and* are the most frequently used three-letter words, and *that* is the most common four-letter word.

When a cryptographer wants to break a code and he thinks that the message is in English, he begins by looking for one- and two-letter words. He notices which code symbols appear most often. He looks for possible double vowels or consonants and for common two-letter and three-letter endings. Incidentally, the three-letter endings most frequently used in English are *-ing, -ion,* and *-ant.*

If the language is not English, the method is the same, but the patterns may vary.

Activities

KN CO
1. Do some research to familiarize yourself with codes. For example, you might read about tick-tack-toe code, triple threat code, Morse code, or Caesar's code. The latter is a **shift code** in which all of the letters are written in order and then shifted a certain number of places, or letters, forward, or to the right.

AN SY
2. On a chart, list and evaluate the codes you read about in activity 1. Which ones would be the easiest to learn? Which ones would be the most difficult to crack? Why?

CO AP
3. Devise a code of some kind and use it to send a message to a friend or classmate.

CO AP AN
4. With computers, it is relatively easy to perform the kind of linguistic analysis described above and to crack a code in which symbols or letters stand for other letters. List ten things that you could do to make a code much more difficult for your enemies to crack *without* making it impossible for your allies to learn or understand.

Solving the Minoan Mystery

Every unknown written language is a kind of secret code. In 1893, British archaeologist Sir Arthur Evans began excavating at Knossos on the Mediterranean island of Crete. He discovered a lost civilization and called it "Minoan" in honor of its mythological king, Minos. Among the remnants Evans found of this ancient civilization were nearly four thousand clay tablets covered with hieroglyphic writing in an unknown script. Evans was aware that the writing matched that on some small engraved stones he had found earlier in Athens, Greece; but he was unable to translate the unknown writing into a familiar language and so was unable to decipher the messages on the tablets.

The man who deciphered the messages on the tablets was Michael Ventris, an English architect. In 1936, as a boy, Ventris had visited an exhibition at which Sir Arthur Evans lectured about Knossos and about the tablets he had found there. Ventris was so inspired by the lecture that he resolved to identify the unknown script, "crack the code," and decipher the messages.

Forced to work without a **bilingual**—that is, a document on which a message is written in both a known and the unknown language—Ventris relied instead on his acquaintance with wartime code-breaking techniques. Meticulously, he analyzed the frequency and relative position of each symbol. During his analysis, Ventris observed that there were too few symbols for the messages to be in picture writing and too many symbols for the unknown script to be an alphabet. Consequently, he concluded that the script with which he was working was a **syllabary**, a set of written symbols or characters that each stood for a different spoken syllable. Ventris then worked out a set of sound values for the symbols which made sense in Greek. In 1953, Michael Ventris's decipherment of the ancient Minoan script was published in the *Journal of Hellenic Studies.*

Linguists have termed the script in which these messages were written **Linear B.** It was derived from an earlier hieroglyphic script and consists of eighty-seven symbols and a number of ideograms. Linear B was in use at Knossos between 1450 and 1400 B.C. Examples of it have also been found in the Mycenaean palaces of Greece. Because of the work of Michael Ventris, the language written in this script has been identified as a primitive form of Greek.

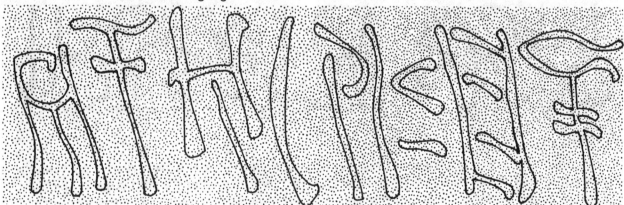

Activities

AP AN 1. Analyze one of the paragraphs on this page to discover which letter appears most often, which is the most common vowel, which is the most common consonant, and which double letters and three-letter endings are used.

AN SY 2. Compare the results of your analysis in activity 1 with the patterns and frequencies described on page 55. In what ways are they similar? In what ways are they different? If you observed several differences, what factors might account for them? How many letters were in your sample? In what ways might the size of your sample have affected your results?

Masks' Messages

When you hear the word *mask,* what do you think of? Do you conjure up images of Halloween, Mardi Gras, costume parties, kabuki players, the ceremonial garb of members of some faraway tribe, or the devices worn by baseball catchers and hockey goalies? Quite simply, a **mask** is an artificial covering for the face or head which is used as a disguise or protection. It may be either fastened to the face, placed over the head, held in front of the face by a handle, or painted directly on the face in the form of makeup.

For thousands of years, people have used masks made of stone, wood, and many other materials for ceremonial, medicinal, protective, religious, and theatrical purposes. For example, scholars believe that a picture of a masked dancer wearing animal horns painted on a cave wall in southern France is more than fifteen thousand years old. Members of some African tribes used masks and costumes to change themselves into good or evil spirits with uncontestable power to cure illnesses, enforce moral codes, and settle disputes. The ancient Egyptians, who looked forward to a pleasurable life after death, made death masks of gold and precious gems, which were entombed with the bodies of the persons they represented. The purpose of these elaborate masks was to preserve the identity of the wearer so that his soul could be recognized by the gods and welcomed by them to the afterlife he had earned.

Masks can be a medium of communication. Think about the message conveyed by a clown's makeup or by the likeness of a witch or a ghost. The clown's painted face may say, "I am a lovable creature at the mercy of life." The witch's mask may say, "I am a nasty old crone just waiting to cast a terrible spell." And the ghost may be friendly or frightening, depending on his facial expression.

Even without covering or makeup, the human face is an expressive medium. It is shaped by a myriad of tiny muscles and is capable of as many as 250,000 different expressions. These expressions may reflect or hide the wearer's feelings. A good actor is the master not only of his voice, but also of his face. He is able to use it to express amusement, anger, fear, joy, puzzlement, sorrow, surprise, and a host of other emotions without moving a limb or uttering a sound.

Masks' Messages Activity Sheet

KN
CO
AP
1. Obtain twenty three-by-five-inch index cards. On each card, write an emotion. For example, you might include **anger, fear, joy, relief, sorrow,** and **surprise.** Put these cards in a coffee can, jar, hat, or other widemouthed container. Working in front of a mirror, draw a card and see how effectively you can use your face to express the emotion named on the card. Or, working with a team, use the cards for a variation on the game charades in which members of one team take turns using their faces to express emotions while members of the other team try to identify these emotions. To make this activity more challenging, set a time limit for each charade and have the actor sit in a chair and place a drape of some sort over his body so that only his face is visible.

KN
CO
AP
2. Do some research to learn more about the traditional use of masks in the Greek or Japanese theater, in North American Indian lore, or in connection with regularly held festivals such as Mardi Gras. What masks are used? What characters, emotions, or spirits are these masks supposed to represent? Share what you learn by drawing a series of illustrations or making several masks. For the latter, use fabric scraps, felt, grocery sacks, paper plates, papier-mâché, tagboard, or other similar materials.

AP
3. Design and make a mask that transforms your personality or changes your identity completely.

AP
4. First, write and learn a monologue that would be appropriate for you to speak while you are wearing the mask you made in activity 3. Then, wear your mask and recite the monologue for the class.

AP
AN
5. Cut out pictures of famous people from old newspapers and magazines. Disguise one of these people by altering the shape of the nose or mouth or by adding a beard, mustache, or sunglasses. When you have finished, show your picture to a friend to see if he or she can recognize the person. From your experience, which facial features seem to be most important for accurate identification?

CO
AN
6. Make a brief list of times when you or others you know might be inclined to use facial expressions to mask, or hide, true feelings.

AN
SY
EV
7. Consider the list you made in activity 6. Is complete honesty *always* the best policy? Are there times when people should mask their true feelings? What happens if they hide their feelings so often that it becomes a habit? Might they have trouble expressing their feelings even when it is appropriate to do so?

Nonverbal Communication

Spoken and written words are not the only ways in which people communicate. Without making a sound or writing a sentence, they share their thoughts and feelings. Using facial expressions, posture, and gestures, people can say that they are afraid, amused, bored, disappointed, happy, sad, shocked, or surprised. This type of sharing is called **nonverbal communication.**

Sometimes, nonverbal communication is used in place of verbal communication, especially when speech is ineffective—perhaps because the communicators do not understand the same language—or inappropriate. Before it was possible to make motion pictures with sound, movie actors could not rely on spoken words to tell their story. Instead, they had to use exaggerated motions and gestures. They became masters of nonverbal communication. For example, Charlie Chaplin could make an audience roar with laughter without uttering a sound. Chaplin's hands, face, characteristic walk, and baggy pants worked together to convey his humorous message. Likewise, pantomime artists such as Marcel Marceau say everything with their faces, hands, and bodies. And a broadcast engineer may nonverbally signal "cut" by drawing his extended index finger across his throat when it would be inappropriate for him to interrupt a program by yelling, "Stop!"

More often, however, nonverbal communication is used with verbal communication. In these instances, expressions, positions, and gestures emphasize, clarify, or nullify the meaning of the spoken message. For example, a speaker may emphasize the importance of a point he is making by pounding the podium with his clinched fist, or a friend may nullify his expression of interest in the story you are telling by turning his attention elsewhere. Although his verbal message is that he wants to hear what you have to say, his nonverbal message is that he is more interested in someone or something else.

Nonverbal communication varies from country to country and from culture to culture. Body positions, facial expressions, and gestures do not have identical meanings throughout the world. For example, when a verbal agreement is made in the United States, the parties to the agreement "seal the deal" with a friendly handshake. In other countries, each party may kiss the other on both cheeks or the parties may slap their hands together. In all of these instances, however, the verbal communication of agreement is reinforced by some sort of nonverbal communication involving body contact.

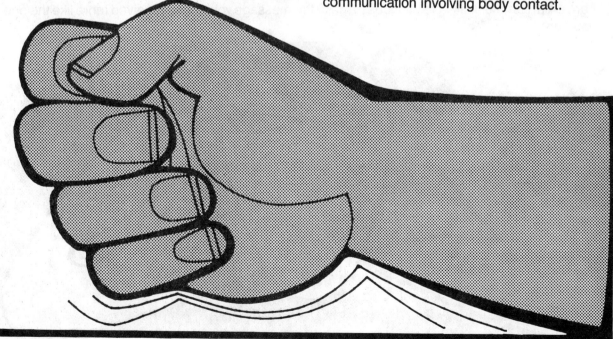

Nonverbal Communication Activity Sheet

KN
CO 1. Do some research to learn how nonverbal communication, which is sometimes called **body language,** varies from country to country and from culture to culture. For example, you might find out how the Japanese or French greet people of whom they are fond. Share what you learn by demonstrating the characteristic gestures and explaining what they mean and when they are used.

KN
CO
AP 2. Practice your body language. Obtain twenty three-by-five-inch index cards. On each card, write an emotion. For example, you might include **anger, boredom, joy, loneliness, rejection, relief, shock, sorrow,** or **surprise.** Put these cards in a coffee can, jar, hat, or other widemouthed container. Working in front of a mirror, draw a card and see how effectively you can use your face and body to express the emotion named on the card. Or, working with a team, use the cards for a variation on the game charades in which members of one team take turns using their faces and bodies to express emotions while members of the other team try to identify these emotions. To make this activity more challenging, set a time limit for each charade.

AN 3. In public places where large groups of strangers gather, people often avoid direct eye contact with one another. Why? What message does direct eye contact communicate? What message is given when someone glances away often during a conversation or avoids eye contact altogether.

AP 4. Obtain twenty three-by-five-inch index cards. On each card, write a simple message that can be expressed in a single sentence. For example, you might write some of the following sentences: **I like you, You are my best friend, I wish you good luck on the test,** or **I missed you when you were absent.** Put these cards in a coffee can, jar, hat, or other widemouthed container. Working with a friend, draw a card and read the message that is written on it. Try to convey this message using only nonverbal methods. Ask your friend to watch you carefully and then to write the message he or she receives on another index card or on a blank sheet of paper.

AN
SY 5. Compare the message you sent in activity 4 with the message your friend received. In what ways are they similar? In what ways are they different? What characteristics of the communication method you used might account for these differences? In what ways might you change your nonverbal communication techniques to make the message your friend received more like the one you sent?

Name _____

Communication Among Animals

Anyone who has owned a dog will tell you that dogs communicate—not with words, of course, but with their barks and their bodies. Sensitive dog owners quickly learn how to distinguish between a yip for food and a whine of pain, between a playful growl and a threatening one. They also learn not to ignore the messages dogs send with their eyes, ears, bodies, and tails and to use both voice tone and body language to communicate effectively with their animals.

Scientists have studied the diverse and ingenious systems animals use to communicate with one another. They have discovered that honeybees use a special wiggle, or "dance," to tell other insects in their hive about the location of food or water. Termites have three distinct ways of warning one another of danger—chemical odors, a scratching sound made with their abdomens, and a curious sequence of movements that resembles a dance. Army ants also use odors for communication. Each colony has its own odor, which is secreted by the queen. If an ant from another colony enters the nest, the intruder will probably be killed because its unfamiliar smell identifies it as an outsider, warns worker ants of approaching danger, and provokes them to attack.

Dolphins communicate with one another by making a variety of sounds that include barks, clicks, and whistles. They use different sounds in response to different events. For example, when the water in which dolphins are swimming is splashed, they make a sound like the creak of a rusty hinge, and each dolphin has its own unique whistle with which it identifies itself to the other members of its school.

Not only do animals have their own languages but they have their own dialects as well. For instance, the sounds made by the Pacific humpback whale differ from those made by the East Coast humpback, and the songs of birds of the same species may vary noticeably when these birds live as little as one hundred miles apart.

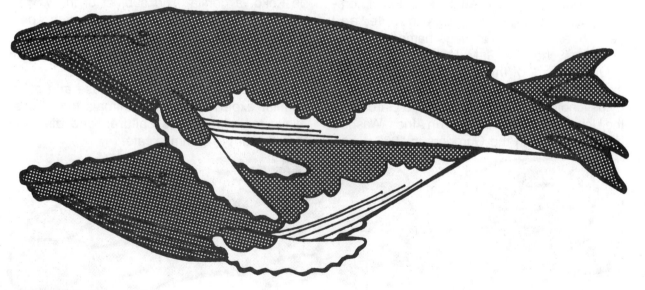

Activities

CO
AP
AN
1. The chemical substances that termites and ants use to communciate are called **pheromones.** These chemicals carry a message and stimulate a predetermined response. Researchers estimate that only ten different pheromones are needed to organize an entire ant colony. List some of the messages ants might communicate in this way.

CO
AP
AN
2. If you have a pet dog or cat, observe its body language. Then draw and label a series of pictures to illustrate at least four distinct messages your pet communicates to you.

Name _____

Talk to the Animals

The fictional Dr. Doolittle was able to talk to the animals. He could speak to each of his animal patients in its own language to ask the nature of its complaint and could understand when the animal described its symptoms. Because of his unique ability to talk to and understand the animals, Dr. Doolittle was able to treat their ailments effectively.

For years, researchers in psycholinguistics have been trying to talk to the animals and to enable animals to talk to them. These scientists have used large marine mammals and primates as the subjects of studies in which they have attempted to learn more about the acquisition and development of language.

At first, researchers tried to teach chimpanzees to talk. When detailed studies of the chimpanzee vocal tract showed that these animals were physically incapable of producing human sounds, scientists began teaching chimps to use and understand artificial and sign languages. Among them were Ameslan, a language of hand signs used as a means of communication primarily by deaf people, and Yerkish, an artificial language named to honor animal psychologist R. M. Yerkes.

One subject of these early communication experiments was Washoe, a chimpanzee owned by psychologists Allen and Beatrice Gardner of the University of Nevada. Born in Africa, Washoe came to live with the Gardners in 1966, when she was only eleven months old. The Gardners treated her like a child. They gave her clothes, toys, and books. Humans stayed with Washoe all day and "chattered" to her in sign language. After seven months, Washoe knew the signs for *give me, more, sweet,* and *up.* A few months later, she combined signs to say *give me sweet.* By the time Washoe was five years old, she had mastered 169 signs and used them constantly to make comments and start conversations. She routinely signed at all humans and even at other animals.

Other chimpanzees have also been taught sign language. Sarah learned to communicate in sign language by manipulating plastic symbols on a magnetic board. Lana used a keyboard to make words appear on a computer screen. These chimps combined elements of sign language in creative ways to tell jokes, express complex emotions, make fun of their human caretakers, and even to lie.

One star language pupil among the primates is Koko, a gorilla. The subject of the world's longest ongoing research project with apes, Koko understands more than one thousand English words and has mastered more than eleven hundred signs.

Psycholinguists are using these and other similar experiments with animals to discover ways to help autistic children and disabled adults learn to communicate.

Activity

CO AP AN Familiarize yourself with American sign language. Learn 42 signs. Record the date on which you learn the first sign, the date on which you learn the last sign, and the number of hours you spend each week practicing. Then compare your learning rate with Washoe's. It took Washoe four years to learn 169 signs. Her average learning rate was 42.25 signs per year. How long did it take you to learn 42 signs? Were you helped or hindered by the fact that you already knew at least one language?

Name _____

Helen Keller

For most children, learning to speak comes as naturally as laughing and crying, but not for children who cannot see or hear. With two major communication pathways eliminated, a person who is both blind and deaf is imprisoned in a dark and silent world. This was the problem faced by Helen Keller and her family.

Helen Adams Keller was born on June 27, 1880, in Tuscumbia, a small town in northern Alabama. She was a happy, healthy baby until, at the age of nineteen months, she fell victim to a mysterious fever that destroyed her sight and hearing. Unable to communicate, Helen became angry and frustrated. She threw her toys, kicked people, and would not let her mother touch her.

In desperation, Helen's mother sought help. Because there was no school for the blind or deaf nearby, Mrs. Keller asked the director of the prestigious Perkins Institution in Boston, Massachusetts, to recommend a qualified teacher.

Twenty-one-year-old Ann Sullivan arrived at the Keller home on March 3, 1887. Believing that Helen had been pampered by her parents because of her multiple handicap, Ann asked to be left alone with the troubled little girl. Ann tried to communicate with Helen by touch. Repeatedly, she "wrote" the finger patterns of the manual alphabet of the deaf on the open palm of Helen's hand. For a time, Helen did not understand. Then one day, beside a water pump, Helen realized that Ann's finger was spelling the name of the cool, refreshing substance she had just felt.

The door to Helen's dark and silent prison had been opened. After that, her progress was rapid. Quickly, she learned to "hear" with the palm of her hand and to "see" with her fingertips. She also learned to write, speak, and use the telephone. In June 1904, she graduated with honors from Radcliffe College in Cambridge, Massachusetts.

Of her limitations Helen Keller wrote, "The marvelous richness of human experience would lose something of rewarding joy if there were no limitations to overcome." By courageously overcoming her own limitations, Helen Keller gained the admiration of people throughout the world and became one of the most effective communicators of her time.

Helen Keller Activity Sheet

KN 1. Look up and learn the meanings of at least ten of the following terms: **amblyopia, cataract, color-blindness, concave, cones, convex, conjunctiva, conjunctivitis, cornea, focal length, focus, glaucoma, hyperopia, image, iris, lens, myopia, night-blindness, ophthalmologist, optician, optometrist, presbyopia, retina, rods, Snellen chart,** and **visual acuity.**

KN
CO 2. Louis Braille, a French organist and teacher of the blind, devised a system of raised-dot writing that makes it possible for sightless people to read with their fingertips. Do some research to learn more about Louis Braille and his remarkable writing system. Share what you learn by means of a brief report.

KN
CO 3. Obtain a Braille alphabet sheet and see how many letters you can learn to recognize by touch alone.

KN
CO 4. Do some research to learn how the human ear collects and amplifies sounds. Share what you learn by means of a labeled diagram.

KN
CO 5. Do some research to learn how the human eye works, what vision problems afflict sighted people, and how optometrists and ophthalmologists correct these problems. Share what you learn by means of a series of labeled diagrams.

KN
CO
AP 6. The eye is a very delicate organ that can be irreparably damaged by injury or illness. Learn about precautions you and your classmates can take to protect your eyes. Make booster buttons, bumper stickers, and/or posters to encourage sight saving and eye safety.

KN
CO
AP
AN 7. Most of us learn by hearing and seeing. Two-thirds of our information about the world comes to us through our eyes. Because Helen Keller was blind, she learned about the world by touching and being touched. She ran her hands over people's faces to learn what they looked like, touched their lips lightly to understand what they said, and "listened" when someone "wrote" on the palm of her hand.

  With your classmates, simulate some of Helen's experiences. Blindfold members of your class and have them identify other members of your class by running their fingers lightly over their classmates' faces. Have some class members silently move their lips to form words or sentences while other blindfolded members of your class try to identify the words or sentences solely by feeling the lip movements. Discuss your experiences and your feelings about them.

KN
CO
AP 8. Try some experiments in which blindfolded students identify objects and substances by touch and/or smell. Put familiar objects of varying shapes and textures in a box or bag and have blindfolded students reach in, pull out an object, and name or describe it without looking at it. Ask blindfolded students to identify fruit and vegetable slices without tasting them.

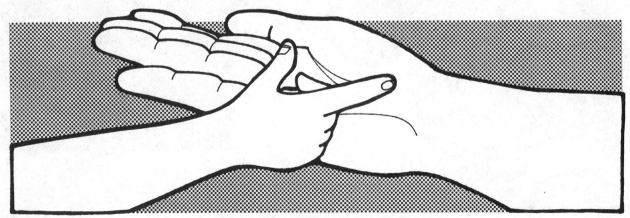

Name _____

Labanotation

The dialogue and stage directions for a play are written in words, the music for a concert is written in notes and rests, and the solution for a calculus problem is written in mathematical symbols. Each of these three areas of human endeavor—theater, music, and mathematics—has its own language. For three hundred years, however, there was no language for dance, no system choreographers could use to describe the sequence of steps and the speed and direction of movements that comprise a ballet.

The choreography of a few great ballets from the past, including *Giselle* (1841) and *Swan Lake* (1877), has been preserved because the traditional movements have been handed down from experienced dancer to novice, from teacher to student. But this method is not very reliable because individual dancers often alter the original choreography to simplify the steps or to give the movements their own interpretation.

Motion pictures would seem to be the simplest way to record a ballet; but films provide an accurate record of the way a ballet is actually performed, not of the way it was originally choreographed. For the reasons described above, dancers sometimes change the steps during a performance; and some movements are so rapid or intricate that they are difficult to capture on film.

During the 1920s, Rudolf von Laban, a choreographer and teacher, decided that a notation system was needed to preserve the great choreographic works for future generations of dancers and to provide an accurate reference for dance historians and researchers. Von Laban devised a dance language in which each movement, its length, speed, and direction, and the part of the body that is used can be adequately described. Known as **Labanotation** after its developer, this language can be used in combination with film or video tape to provide a complete and accurate record of a ballet. It is flexible enough to be adapted for use in describing changing dance styles and is comprehensive enough to be understood and used by choreographers in all fields of dance throughout the world.

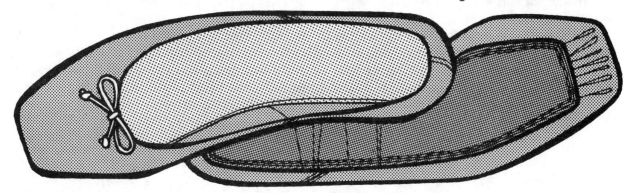

Activities

KN 1. Look up and learn the meanings of at least ten of the following ballet terms: **adagio, allegro, arabesque, arabesque allongée, attitude, attitude derrière, attitude devant, ballerina, barre, corps de ballet, danseur, entrechat, jeté, pas de deux, pirouette, plié, sur les pointes, tour en l'air,** and **tour jeté.**

KN CO 2. From which language does much of the vocabulary used to describe the ballet come? Why?

AN SY 3. Some sports, such as baseball and football, have a system for diagramming or writing the plays of the game. Compare one of these systems with Labanotation. In what ways are they similar? In what ways are they different? Is it possible to recreate an entire game or ballet from the notation alone? Explain your answer.

Technological Advances in Communication

Since the dawn of human history, people have sought ways to communicate and ways to improve communication. Cro-Magnons painted pictures on cave walls. Ancient Hawaiians used conch shells to send warnings. Maya priests carved calendar glyphs in stone disks. Although we think of technology in terms of automation, industrialization, and specialization, these early changes in the means of communication may be classified as technological advances because each one represented the application of a new or different technique to make the communication process faster, easier, and/or more efficient.

Among the many technological advances that have improved the means and methods of communication, none was more important than the invention and refinement of printing. In Europe during the Middle Ages, some people could read, but only a privileged few had access to books. Because books had to be copied by hand, they were extremely scarce and were usually kept in private libraries. Ordinary people had little opportunity to own or read them.

For many years, printers in China and Korea had printed with blocks. In A.D. 1034, Pi Sheng invented movable type made of baked clay, but his method did not gain widespread popularity. Many Chinese printers were comfortable with the old block method, which seemed well suited to printing a language written chiefly in stylized pictures.

By the fifteenth century, more and more people wanted books. Neither the European method of hand copying nor the Oriental one of block printing was fast enough to keep up with the increasing demand. Around A.D. 1450, Johann Gutenberg, working in his shop in Mainz, Germany, perfected the process of printing from movable metal type. Between 1450 and 1455, he used this process to produce a two-volume, 1,282-page edition of the Bible.

Printing was faster than hand copying, but this process was still relatively slow. Each page of a book had to be printed individually on a separate sheet of paper. It was at least three hundred years before additional technological advances made it possible for books to be mass produced. First, a machine was invented that could make paper in continuous rolls. Next, around 1848, Richard March Hoe, the son of a printing press manufacturer, invented a rotary press. With this remarkable machine, movable metal type could be arranged on a cylinder that revolved and was inked automatically as paper from rolls was fed through. Finally, the invention of rotary presses that could print in color and of machines that could fold, bind, and trim made it possible for books to be mass produced and for ordinary people to own them.

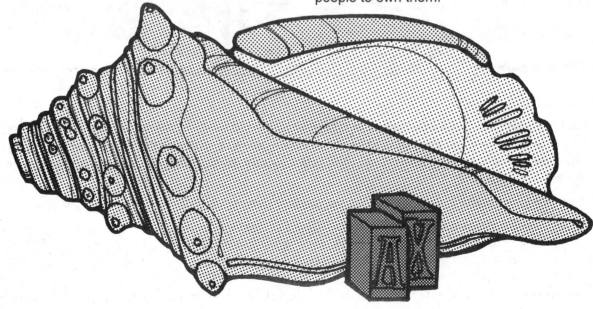

Name _____

Technological Advances in Communication
Activity Sheet

KN
CO
1. Choose one of the following methods of communication: books, bumper stickers, computers, film, magazines, megaphones, newspapers, posters, telephones, television, or videotape. Using pictures cut from magazines and newspapers or original drawings, create a montage that illustrates the ways in which this method has been and/or is being used.

KN
CO
2. Do some research to learn more about the following names and terms: **boldface, colophon, compositor, copyright, cut, cutline, edition, folio, font, gutter, holiday, italic, justification, lead, Linotpye, manuscript, margin, Ottmar Mergenthaler, monk, offset, pica, point, quarto, recto, roman, scribe, spine, typeface, typeset,** and **verso.** For each one, write its definition and then explain its significance in the history of book reproduction or the process of printing.

AP
AN
3. In the earliest form of printing, a hand-carved wooden block was used as the plate. First, the necessary letters were drawn on the surface of the block. Second, the surrounding wood was carefully cut away from these letters. Next, a thin, even coat of ink was spread on the raised letters. Then, a sheet of paper was laid on the inked wooden block, smoothed, and rubbed. Finally, the sheet was peeled away from the block and laid flat or hung up to dry. As you might imagine, this kind of printing—block printing—was a very slow process.

   Using linoleum, vegetables, or wood, experiment with block printing. If you had to rely on this method, how long would it take you to prepare the necessary blocks and print a classroom newspaper?

KN
CO
4. Before such modern technological advances as the telephone and radio, telegraph, flags, smoke, and blinking lights were used to send messages by means of visual signals. During the 1790s, French engineers Claude and Ignace Urbain Chappe invented an extensively used telegraph system that employed visual signals. Within fifty years, the Chappe telegraph network connected twenty-nine French cities through five hundred stations. These stations were located in towers atop hills that were approximately five miles apart. Signals were flashed by operators along the line of sight from one tower to the next. Using a map, locate some well-known "telegraph hills" in France, the United States, or elsewhere.

AN
SY
EV
5. With this visual telegraph system, it took fifteen minutes for a message to be relayed over a distance of five hundred miles. Compare the visual and radio telegraph systems. In what ways are they similar? In what ways are they different? Which one would be faster? Which one would be more reliable? How reliable would a communication system based on visual signals be during a dense fog? Which one would be more accurate?

Name _____

Out-of-This-World Technology

During the past several decades, scientific research has provided us with additional technological advances in the area of communication. Voice-activated computers, talking robots, and "interactive television," with instantaneous two-way viewing, are already on the market. Fiber optics and specialized satellites are being used to provide even more channels for communication.

One of the newest technological advances in communication is the Airfone, an air-to-ground system used by passengers aboard commercial airliners. Not content with sending messages from air to ground or earth to sky, physicists are currently experimenting with methods for sending messages deep into space.

In 1972, scientists launched Pioneer 10 en route to the stars. The message carried aboard this space probe was designed by Carl Sagan, a professor of astronomy at Cornell University, and is written in scientific notation. It is intended to acquaint the interstellar civilization that finds it with our planet, earth.

Voyagers 1 and 2, which are also space probes, each carry a phonograph record designed to last a billion years. Written on each record jacket in scientific notation are instructions for playing the record and information about the position and present epoch of the earth. On the records themselves are greetings in fifty languages, a message from former President Jimmy Carter, and the sounds of rain, of people, and of cars.

Using space probes to send recorded messages into interstellar space is one thing, but making telephone calls over interstellar distances is quite another. Before these long-distance calls can become a reality, researchers will have to find a communication signal that can be easily distinguished from the natural static of space. This signal must be easy to generate and detect, and it should require as little power as possible.

Although light waves, microwaves, and radio waves are all candidates to become interstellar message carriers, scientists are also considering neutrinos. First detected in 1953, **neutrinos** are particles that travel at the speed of light and can easily pass through dust clouds, planets, or other obstructing masses. Neutrino telephones for interstellar communication may be built early in the twenty-first century. Scientists warn, however, that the hardest part of interstellar communication is not developing the technology, but finding a language the recipients can understand.

Activity

CO AP 1. In 1950, people on earth started trying to detect possible interstellar transmissions from other civilizations inhabiting our galaxy. So far, the search has been unsuccessful, but most significant wavelengths and many regions of the sky remain unstudied. Imagine that you are the lucky astronomer who first detects intelligible signals from outer space. Make an entry in your journal in which you identify the origin of these signals, translate the message being sent, and describe your feelings at being able to receive and understand it.

Name _____

Communications as a Career

Communications has become a popular major field of study and career choice among students on college and university campuses. Educational institutions offering degrees in communications usually structure the required course work to create an interdisciplinary field of study and/or an interdepartmental major. For example, students wishing to earn a degree in communications may be required to take courses in biology, computer science, economics, English, history, journalism, linguistics, political science, psychology, sociology, and speech. They need to know how people hear and learn to speak, how language develops and reflects culture, and how messages are received and understood so that their own messages will be effective.

Students who graduate with a degree in communications become investigative reporters, write feature articles for newspapers, and/or anchor television news programs. They also do public relations work for government and community groups and for hospitals and health maintenance organizations. Depending on their additional areas of advanced study and scientific specialization, they may also act as consultants to solve communications problems for large corporations or as therapists to aid individuals whose normal channels of communication have been impaired.

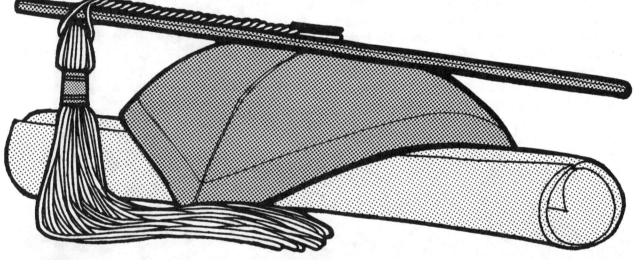

Activities

KN CO 1. Contact a college or university to learn more about communications as a field of study. Find out what courses a communications major is required to take and what additional courses are recommended. Also find out what career opportunities await a college graduate with a degree in this field. Share what you learn by means of a list, table, or chart.

KN CO 2. If possible, interview someone whose career is in the communications field. Ask that person what his duties and responsiblities are, why he chose this field, and what education and experience prepared him for this career. Also ask what recommendations he would make to a young person wishing to pursue a similar career. If possible, tape record your interview and play it for the class. If not, write a brief report in which you summarize what you learned from the interview.

AP 3. Pretend that you intend to be a communications major at a specific college or university. Using a general catalog from that institution, select courses and plan your schedule for four years of study. As you do so, keep in mind the general college requirements, the specific requirements of your major, and any prerequisites (that is, lower division courses that you *must* take before you will be allowed to take upper division courses that you *want* to take).

Correlated Activities

CO AP Make a time line detailing the development of paper. Begin with papyrus and conclude with the specialized products of today, including xerographic and No-Carbon-Required (NCR) papers.

AP One of the greatest advances in communication was development of the newspaper. Put together a class or school newspaper. Make it your goal to improve communication between two specific groups, such as students in one room and students in another, students and teachers, students in two different schools, or students at school and parents at home.

KN CO Do some research to discover how the American Indian, Greek, Japanese, and Mexican cultures have used masks in the past. Do these groups still use masks today? If so, in what ways?

AN SY Does wearing a mask affect the way you behave? Experiment by performing a skit in front of your class twice, once with a mask and once without. Discuss the differences in your actions and feelings.

CO AP Using original drawings or pictures cut from catalogs and magazines, compile and label a fashion portfolio of clothing that (1) makes a personal statement, (2) makes a political statement, (3) expresses status, and (4) expresses membership in a group.

Correlated Activities
(continued)

AP
AN Sighted people acquire at least two-thirds of their information about the world by *seeing* it. What happens to someone who is visually impaired? Working with a partner for safety, experience some of the challenges and frustrations that a visually impaired person experiences by wearing a blindfold while you make a sandwich, make a telephone call, or make change for a dollar. Discuss your experiences and your feelings about them.

AN Read the Hindu fable entitled "The Blind Men and the Elephant." Analyze this fable. What is the real cause of the misperception or misunderstanding described in this story? Is it physical blindness or is it a form of mental, or intellectual, blindness that makes the men accept without question a small part of the elephant as the whole elephant, a small part of the truth as the whole truth? Can you think of other instances in which confusing a part with the whole might impair communication or prevent understanding?

AN
SY Select one communication medium. List five ways in which it has influenced individuals or nations. In what ways would you change this medium or its uses so that it would serve people better?

AP
AN The glyphs on Maya stelae and the hieroglyphs on Egyptian pyramids are gradually being eroded. Read about this problem. Then, devise a way to protect these and other historical stone monuments from the effects of time, weather, and pollution.

CO
AP Pick a feeling or emotion and express it in two of the following ways; acting, dancing, drawing, painting, pantomiming, sculpting, and writing prose or poetry.

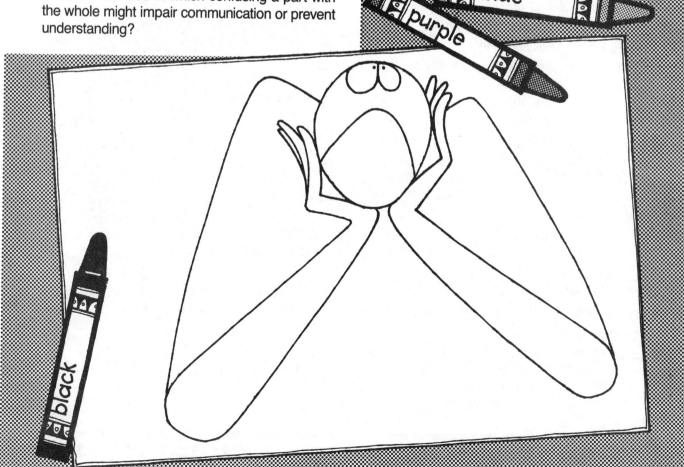

Name _____

Postest

Circle the letter beside the best answer or the most appropriate response.

1. **Papyrus** is a
   a. tufted marsh plant.
   b. Babylonian city.
   c. communications satellite.
   d. computer program.

2. *Acta Diurna* (Daily Events) was
   a. a personal diary kept by a Roman soldier.
   b. the first regularly published newspaper in Europe.
   c. a newssheet posted in Rome, Italy, in 59 B.C.
   d. a manuscript copied by a European monk.

3. Old English was permanently influenced by the language spoken by
   a. the Celts.
   b. the Romans.
   c. the Scandinavians.
   d. all of the above.

4. Benjamin Harris of Boston, Massachusetts,
   a. perfected the process of printing from movable metal type.
   b. published the first newspaper in colonial America.
   c. published the first daily newspaper in England.
   d. invented a telegraph system that used visual signals.

5. In 1822, Jean François Champollion
   a. made the first photograph.
   b. produced pencil lead.
   c. developed a universal language.
   d. translated hieroglyphs.

6. Polish linguist Lazarus Ludwig Zamenhof developed
   a. the printing press.
   b. an artificial language.
   c. an ethnic dialect.
   d. a system of dance notation.

7. **Labanotation** is a
   a. universal language.
   b. system of mathematical symbols.
   c. collection of signs, notes, and rests used to write music.
   d. system for recording all of the movements in a dance.

8. Pantomimists are masters of
   a. oral communication.
   b. nonverbal communication.
   c. written communication.
   d. costumes and makeup.

9. **Pasigraphy** is
   a. an international picture language.
   b. calligraphy written on papyrus.
   c. the art of manuscript illumination.
   d. a universal spoken language.

10. **Pheromone** is a
    a. hormone produced when one is afraid.
    b. universal spoken language.
    c. chemical substance with which animals communicate.
    d. sign language used primarily by deaf people.

Answer Key

Pretest, Page 34

1. d	6. b
2. c	7. b
3. b	8. a
4. d	9. c
5. d	10. d

Posttest, Page 72

1. a	6. b
2. c	7. d
3. d	8. b
4. b	9. a
5. d	10. c

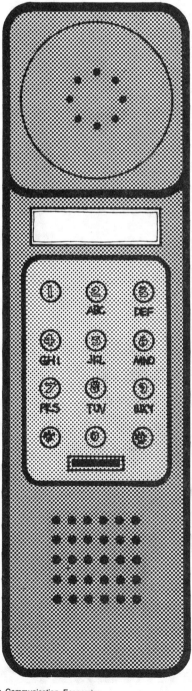
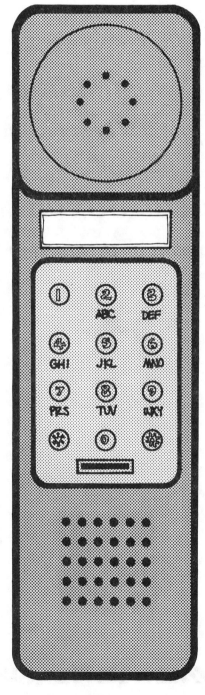
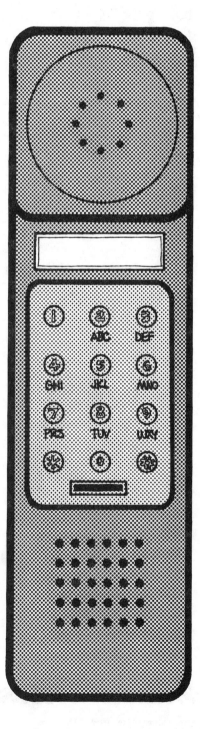

This is to certify that

_____
(name of student)

has satisfactorily completed a unit of study

on

Communication

and has been named

a

Competent Communicator

in recognition of this accomplishment.

_____
<small>(signature of teacher)</small>

_____
<small>(date)</small>

Economics

Bulletin Board Ideas

THE STORY OF MONEY

PAST   PRESENT   FUTURE

Instructions: Print or cut out letters to spell the title **The Story of Money** and the headings **Past, Present,** and **Future.** Pin, staple, or tack these headings on a bulletin board as shown. Below the **Past** heading, post pictures of beads, ancient coins, grain, salt, skins, and wampum. Below the **Present** heading, post pictures or photocopies of domestic and foreign coins and currency. Explain to students that the future of money will depend on what people of the future choose to use as a method of payment, a medium of exchange, and a store of value. Encourage students to draw pictures depicting their ideas about the forms money may take in the future and post them on the board under the **Future** heading.

EARLY ECONOMIC MILESTONES

600 B.C.	STATE COINAGE ORIGINATED IN LYDIA.
A.D. 1272	THE CHINESE EMPEROR KUBLA KHAN ISSUED CURRENCY PRINTED ON PAPER MADE FROM MULBERRY TREE BARK.
A.D. 1587	THE BANCO DELLA PIAZZA WAS OPENED IN VENICE, ITALY.
A.D. 1652	JOHN HULL, A GOLDSMITH AND SILVERSMITH, BECAME MANAGER OF THE FIRST AMERICAN COLONIAL MINT, WHICH WAS LOCATED IN THE MASSACHUSETTS BAY COLONY.
A.D. 1792	THE FIRST UNITED STATES MINT WAS ESTABLISHED.
A.D. 1945	THE WORLD BANK, HEADQUARTERED IN WASHINGTON, D.C., OPENED ITS DOORS.

Instructions: Print or cut out letters to spell the title **Early Economic Milestones.** Pin, staple, or tack this title on a bulletin board as shown. Cut rectangular strips of tagboard. Select five or six of these strips and print a date and related event on each one. Post these strips on the board in chronological order. Make available blank strips of tagboard and black felt-tipped marking pens. Encourage students to add their own economic date discoveries to this display.

Learning Center Ideas

THE MAGIC OF GOLD

GOLD IS NO LONGER USED AS AN EVERYDAY METHOD OF PAYMENT OR MEDIUM OF EXCHANGE, BUT THIS SHINY METAL HAS CAPTURED THE IMAGINATIONS OF PEOPLE THROUGHOUT HISTORY. THEY HAVE SEARCHED FOR IT, KILLED FOR IT, DIED FOR IT, USED IT, ABUSED IT, AND EVEN SOUGHT TO TURN OTHER SUBSTANCES INTO IT BY BOTH CHEMISTRY AND SORCERY. TO LEARN MORE ABOUT THIS INTRIGUING SUBSTANCE, COMPLETE AT LEAST TWO OF THE ACTIVITIES DESCRIBED BELOW.

LEARN MORE ABOUT THE CHEMICAL AND PHYSICAL PROPERTIES OF GOLD. FOR EXAMPLE, IS IT AN ELEMENT OR A COMPOUND? WHAT IS ITS CHEMICAL SYMBOL? WHY? IS IT HARD OR SOFT? DOES IT COMBINE READILY WITH OTHER ELEMENTS?

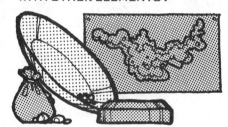

DO RESEARCH ON ONE OF THE FOLLOWING TOPICS. SHARE WHAT YOU LEARN BY MEANS OF CHARTS, DRAWINGS, MAPS, A REPORT, AND/OR A SKIT.

• ALCHEMY
• BURIED TREASURE
• FORT KNOX
• GOLD MINES
• THE GOLD RUSH
• GOLD TEETH
• JEWELRY
• THE SEVEN CITIES OF CÍBOLA
• KING TUTANKHAMON

FUTURE SPACE TRAVELERS MIGHT FIND GOLD ON MERCURY, VENUS, OR MARS. WRITE A STORY ABOUT A "GOLD RUSH" TO ANOTHER PLANET. INCLUDE ILLUSTRATIONS.

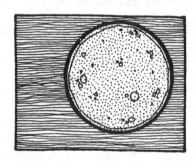

THE BUSINESS SECTION

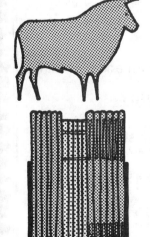

AT THIS CENTER YOU CAN

• READ THE BUSINESS SECTION OF THE NEWSPAPER.
• STUDY THE FINANCIAL PAGES OF THE NEWSPAPER.
• EXPLORE FORBES, FORTUNE, AND MONEY MAGAZINES.
• CHECK RECENT STOCK MARKET REPORTS.
• PLOT THE MOOD AND HEALTH OF THE MARKET.

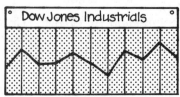

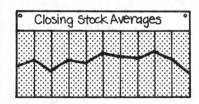

Name _____

Pretest

Circle the letter beside the best answer or the most appropriate response.

1. The study of how people use their resources to meet their needs and satisfy their wants, and of how they decide to distribute the goods and services they acquire and produce is called
   a. consumerism.
   b. advertising.
   c. economics.
   d. marketing.

2. Anyone who buys goods and services is called
   a. a shopper.
   b. a consumer.
   c. a producer.
   d. an economist.

3. The process in which one thing is exchanged for another is called
   a. economics.
   b. production.
   c. investment.
   d. barter.

4. Anything that is given or received in return for goods and services is called
   a. coins.
   b. money.
   c. currency.
   d. credit.

5. Historians believe that state coinage originated during the seventh century B.C. in
   a. Lydia.
   b. Egypt.
   c. Greece.
   d. Rome.

6. The first currency was printed on paper made from mulberry tree bark by the
   a. Egyptians.
   b. Minoans.
   c. Chinese.
   d. Greeks.

7. Adam Smith, in his study entitled *Inquiry into the Nature and Causes of the Wealth of Nations*, advocated natural liberty of trade and commerce in which economies would be driven by self-interest and regulated by
   a. government.
   b. tariffs.
   c. taxes.
   d. competition.

8. When Henry Ford reduced automobile production time by using conveyor belts and improved assembly line methods, the price of a Ford Model T
   a. dropped from $850 in 1908 to approximately $400 in 1916.
   b. remained the same because workers' wages rose.
   c. remained the same because steel prices rose.
   d. increased because of rising wages and steel prices, but not much.

9. On October 29, 1929, following a decade of unprecedented economic growth and unhealthy speculation, the Stock Market crashed. This means that
   a. a large commercial building collapsed, severely injuring many of its occupants.
   b. corporations withdrew stock offerings from the market.
   c. stock prices went down drastically, and people who had invested in stocks lost a lot of money.
   d. investment brokers staged an organized boycott of the market.

10. Economies experience cycles of expansion and contraction. By 1976, the United States economy was
    a. improving after a mild recession.
    b. recovering from a deep depression.
    c. in its worst slump in more than thirty years.
    d. the healthiest it had been in more than thirty years.

Name _____

What Is Economics?

Economics is the study of how people use their resources to meet their needs and satisfy their wants, and of how they decide to distribute and consume the goods and services they acquire and produce. The overall structure within which economic activity takes place is called an **economy.** People who study economies are called **economists.** They have two main purposes for their study. Their first purpose is to understand how an economy works and to explain the ways in which factors and forces within the economy are related. Their second purpose is to use this knowledge to prevent or solve economic problems.

In studying economies, economists focus their attention on four distinct entities: the producer, the consumer, the market, and the prevailing philosophy or applicable regulations. For purposes of economics, a **producer** is anyone who makes goods or provides services. A **con-** **sumer** is anyone who buys goods and services. The **market** is the place or atmosphere in which goods are sold or exchanged, or the mechanism by which this exchange is accomplished. The market operates according to a certain philosophy. It is influenced by the attitudes of producers and consumers, and is controlled by government actions and regulations.

Economists use certain tools to help them understand the past, analyze the present, and predict the future of economies. One of these tools is **economic data,** which are facts and figures regarding the economy collected by both government and private groups. Another of these tools is an economic model. In this instance, a **model** is a set of data presented as a mathematical representation of a system. Thus, an **economic model** is a framework within which economists can organize, examine, and use data representing an economic system.

Activities

KN
CO
1. Read the business section or financial pages of your newspaper. Find at least five words that are new to you. Print each of these words on one side of a three-by-five-inch index card. Look up the definitions of these words and print them on the backs of the cards. Alphabetize the cards, put a rubber band around them, and keep them as the beginning of a pocket dictionary of economic terms. Create new cards as you encounter additional unfamiliar words.

KN
CO
2. In any one situation, some people are producers and others are consumers; but in a different situation, these roles may be reversed. For example, a farmer is a producer of food; but he is also a consumer of food and of clothing, fertilizer, gasoline, tires, and tools as well. Make a table or chart on which you list five producers of goods and/or services. Below each producer, list some of the goods and services he or she consumes.

Name _____

Economic Headlines, 1776–1976

Certain historical events have influenced the economic growth of the United States. The headlines recorded on this page and on page 81 highlight a few of these events.

1776
Adam Smith Publishes
Wealth of Nations

In 1776, Adam Smith, a Scottish political economist, published a study entitled *Inquiry into the Nature and Causes of the Wealth of Nations.* In this study, Smith described a theory of division of labor, money, prices, wages, and distribution, and advocated a natural liberty of trade and commerce, which he said would be driven by self-interest and regulated by competition. His ideas became authoritative in politics as well as economics and still have a strong influence on economic thinking throughout the world.

1790
First Industrial Factory
Built in United States

In 1790, Samuel Slater built the first successful water-powered cotton mill in the United States. This mill was located on the Blackstone River in Pawtucket, Rhode Island, a town in which textile manufacture remains the most important industry.

1825
Erie Canal Completed

In 1825, the last section of the Erie Canal was completed. This canal extended more than 350 miles, from Albany to Buffalo, New York, and connected the Hudson River with Lake Erie. Thus, it linked the Atlantic coastal states with the Great Lakes region.

1836
Model Town Built

In 1836, Lowell, Massachusetts, was incorporated as a town. It had begun to develop after textile mills were built on the Merrimack River at the confluence of the Concord in 1822. The town contained homes, schools, churches, and social halls. Life in Lowell was much nicer than in most other mill towns of that time.

1857
Iron Bridge Spans
Green River

In 1857, an iron-and-steel bridge was completed over the Green River in Tennessee. No longer would rivers and canyons prevent the laying of railroad track or stand in the way of westward movement and economic growth.

1862
Innovation Spurs
Steel Industry

In the 1860s, an increased demand for steel made it necessary to find a way to make this metal quickly and cheaply. In answer to this demand, Americans developed a system that combined the best features of the methods invented earlier by Englishman Sir Henry Bessemer and American William Kelly. In the Bessemer process, steel was manufactured by decarbonizing melted pig iron by means of a blast of air. Kelly invented a converter which utilized an air blast on molten iron and the natural carbon content of molten cast iron to obtain greater heat for the process.

Economic Headlines, 1776–1976
(continued)

1908
Model T Changes American Life

In 1908, Henry Ford introduced a relatively inexpensive automobile, the Model T. During the next eight years, he implemented a system of conveyor belts and improved assembly line methods to cut production time for a single vehicle from 12½ hours to 1½ hours. Because of these more efficient production methods, the cost of a Model T dropped from $850 in 1908 to $400 in 1916. The Model T and other automobiles built during this era increased the demand for roads and ultimately hastened the movement of the American people from the cities to the suburbs.

1929
Stock Market Plunges

The Stock Market Crash of 1929 followed a decade of unprecedented economic growth and unhealthy speculation. Businesses failed, and unemployment rose. More than five thousand banks and eighty-five thousand businesses closed their doors forever. One-fourth of the labor force was out of work. The nation's economy fell to an all-time low.

1933
Government Begins Construction Of Grand Coulee Dam

In 1933, the federal government began construction of Grand Coulee Dam on the Columbia River in the state of Washington. The purpose of this dam was to harness the Columbia's waters for power, irrigation, and flood control. The dam, which went into operation in 1941, is one of the largest in the world. It measures 4,300 feet long and stands 550 feet high. The hydroelectric power produced by the power plant at the dam gave an enormous boost to the nation's sagging economy. By building the dam, the government took an active role in promoting present economic recovery and future economic stability.

1970
Inflation Becomes A Worldwide Problem

In 1970, the specter of inflation hung over the United States and the rest of the world. Spiraling prices drove workers to demand higher wages which, in turn, drove prices even higher. The inflation rate rose to 12.4 percent, and the prime interest rate skyrocketed to a record 21 percent. Producers ceased to build, and consumers ceased to buy because neither one could borrow at an affordable rate. By 1976, the nation was in the worst economic slump in more than thirty years.

Economic Headlines of the Future

CO
AP
After reading the headlines and related articles on pages 80 and 81, create some future economic headlines and articles for the spaces below. Consider the ways in which technological developments and space travel may change the supply of goods and services, and the demand for them.

```
┌─────────────────────────────────────────────────────┐
│                                                       │
│  THE ECONOMIC MONITOR                                 │
│                                                       │
│  WASHINGTON, D.C., U.S.A.        SOME FUTURE DATE      │
│                                                       │
│  _____      _____                │
│  _____      _____                │
│  _____      _____                │
│  _____      _____                │
│  _____      _____                │
│  _____      _____                │
│  _____      _____                │
│  _____      _____                │
│  _____      _____                │
│  _____      _____                │
│  _____      _____                │
│  _____      _____                │
│  _____      _____                │
│                                                       │
└─────────────────────────────────────────────────────┘
```

Name _____

Barter

Before anyone thought of money, trade was conducted by means of a process called barter. **Bartering** is exchanging one item for another. To barter, you must first find someone who has something you want and who wants something you have. Then, the two of you must agree on a fair rate of exchange. In barter transactions, no money is used.

Bartering probably began in prehistoric times with the cave dwellers. Some men were better at making tools and weapons while other men excelled at hunting and fishing. The toolmakers traded the extra tools they made for the food they needed. Egyptian hieroglyphics indicate that these ancient people bartered. Even today, some people trade the surplus items they have for the goods and services they want or need.

Barter sounds simple, but it can be a very complicated process. In fact, there are at least three problems inherent in this process: (1) the problem of matching goods or services wanted with goods or services offered so that a direct exchange can be made; (2) the problem of determining a fair and equitable rate of exchange between two very dissimilar items; and (3) the problem of storing value for a period of time.

To understand these problems, imagine a farmer who has too many cows and too few chickens, and wants to trade one cow for some chickens. First, he must find another farmer who has surplus chickens and is willing to trade a certain number of those chickens for a cow. Then, the farmer with the cow and the farmer with the chickens must agree on a rate of exchange.

How many chickens does it take to equal one cow? Do you calculate the relative value of these animals on the basis of weight? egg and milk production? potential for producing offspring? For example, what if the first farmer thought his cow was worth twenty chickens, but the farmer with the chickens offered only ten? Of course, the farmer with the cow could negotiate for something else, but he probably would not be willing to trade half of his cow for half as many chickens as he had expected to receive.

What is the value of half a cow? Your answer to this question will depend very much on how you intend to *use* the cow. If you plan to *eat* the cow, then the value of the animal depends on the amount of meat, or the weight; and half a cow may be worth exactly half what a whole cow is worth. But if you plan to *milk* the cow, then half a cow is worth nothing!

Activities

KN
CO
1. Many newspapers have a **Swap or Trade** section within their classified ads. Read this section in your local newspaper. List the products and services that are being traded and, where possible, indicate the value that is being placed on each.

CO
AN
2. Write a brief paragraph in which you describe a trade you made. Did you have difficulty striking a deal? Were you satisfied with the results? Why or why not?

AN
SY
3. With your parents' permission, bring to class some small toys or craft items you are willing to trade. Make deals with several classmates to exchange your items for theirs. When you have finished trading, take a few minutes to discuss how relative values were determined, how exchange rates were set, why certain trades were made, and what difficulties you encountered.

Name _____

Money

What do you think of when someone says the word *money*? Do you think of the coins jingling in your pocket or of the paper bills folded safely in your wallet? Minted coins and printed currency are forms of money, but money is not limited to these things. Money is anything that is given or received in return for goods or services. It is anything that is used as a **medium of exchange.**

In the past, many things have been used as money. Primitive money was closely related to the livelihood of the people who used it. For example, hunters used skins for money, and farmers used grains. Barley was the first acceptable form of money in Mesopotamia. In ancient Rome, both cattle and salt served as money. In Newfoundland, where fishing is a major industry, codfish were once used as money. Feathers, ivory, shells, stones, tea, and tobacco have all been used as money by different groups of people at different times.

No matter what is used as money, it must exist in only limited supply. If an item used as money becomes too common or too plentiful, it loses its value. For example, in America, strings of beads made from shells were once used as money by the Indians. Called **wampum,** these strings of beads varied in value according to their color. The darker ones were far more highly prized. While the beads were made by hand, there were relatively few of them; and wampum derived a part of its value from its rarity. But soon some enterprising settlers learned how to make these beads and set up factories in New York and New Jersey to mass produce them. The resulting large quantities of wampum made it useless as money because it was no longer considered valuable.

For money to be efficient, it must meet certain criteria. For example, it must be accepted both by the people doing the buying and by the people doing the selling. It must be portable and have a high value for its weight. It must be easily divided into small units, and it must be difficult to counterfeit.

For money to be effective, it must act as a **store of value,** that is, it must have a certain recognized value and retain that value over an extended period of time. For purposes of trade, the value of money must not change with its age or condition. An old, wrinkled dollar bill must be worth the same amount and buy as many goods and services as a crisp, new dollar bill.

All primitive forms of money had serious shortcomings. For example, it was not very convenient to carry around sacks of barley, which were heavy in relation to their value. A cow was impossible to divide into smaller units and difficult to transport over long distances. The value of cows, chickens, and other living things varied with their age and condition. Shells were light, impossible to counterfeit, and not inclined to deteriorate; but they were not rare enough and eventually lost their value and became useless as money and useful only as personal decoration.

Activities

AP AN 1. Think of one school subject in which you are quite good. Imagine that, because of illness and absence from school, a friend of yours has fallen behind in this subject and has asked you to tutor him. You agree to do so. The friend says that he cannot pay you for your time but offers to compensate you in some other way. List ten ways you might suggest. Be certain that each one involves an investment of personal time or use of a valued item but does not require payment in money.

AN EV 2. List some things that are considered valuable by your friends and relatives. Then evaluate several of these things against the criteria described above for money. Could any of these "valuable" things be used as money if you did not have coins or currency? Why or why not?

Name _____

From Goldsmiths to Banks

Banks existed in Babylon more than four thousand years ago and in Greece two thousand years ago. In ancient Rome, one of the streets near the Forum became a bankers' row. For about three hundred years, Florence, Italy, was the main banking city for the world. In fact, the English word **bank** comes from the Old Italian word *banca,* meaning bench. At one time, bankers sat on benches behind tables to take deposits, make loans, and keep accounts.

Banking as we know it probably got its start in Europe during the fifteenth and sixteenth centuries. At that time, gold was used as money. This gold was in the form of coins or blocks of specific weights. Because of robbers and bandits, it was unwise to store a large amount of gold at home or to carry it when one traveled.

The only people who had a good security system were goldsmiths. They stored their gold in vaults and even hired guards to protect it. For this reason, people began to take their gold to goldsmiths for safekeeping. In other words, they **deposited** their gold with a goldsmith for protection and **withdrew** their gold when they needed it for making a payment or purchase.

Before long, depositors realized that they did not need to go to the goldsmith in person to withdraw their gold or to transfer it as payment for a purchase. Instead, all a man really needed to do was give the person from whom he was making the purchase, the seller, a note telling the goldsmith to give the bearer a specified amount of gold from his account. The note was a kind of **check** authorizing the withdrawal of funds or the transfer of gold from one account to another.

Most depositors seldom visited the vault to see if their gold was still there. Goldsmiths noticed that they had large quantities of gold sitting idle and realized that they could make money by lending some of the deposited gold to local entrepreneurs, who needed additional capital. When goldsmiths made these loans, they gambled that not all of their depositors would demand their gold at the same time. If they had, the **reserves** (that is, the amount of gold immediately available to depositors) would not have been sufficient to meet their demands, and the goldsmiths would have been faced with some extremely angry depositors.

Activities

CO 1. Explain what might have happened if all of the depositors had arrived at a goldsmith's shop to claim their gold at the same time or on the same day.

CO
AP 2. Goldsmiths made money by charging **interest** to businessmen on the money they borrowed. Before long, depositors of substantial sums wanted to receive interest on the amount they deposited. Do some research to learn how interest was figured on loans and deposits several hundred years ago. Make a chart or graph in which you compare these rates with current ones.

CO 3. Federally chartered banks are strictly regulated by an agency of the government. Among other things, this agency sets the interest rates for certain types of deposits and determines the reserves that these banks must keep on hand. For this reason, banks cannot be very creative in certain aspects of their operation and may appear very similar. To attract depositors, they offer a variety of special services. Do some research to discover what these services are.

AP 4. Create a brochure in which you use a combination of the services you discovered in activity 3 to promote a fictitious bank.

Coins

Barter was cumbersome. It was difficult to carry large quantities of fish, grain, or skins from place to place and even more difficult to agree on their value. As trade activity increased, it became necessary to find or create a convenient medium of exchange.

Many groups of people used metals for this purpose. Sometimes, these people fashioned gold, silver, or copper into jewelry or plates; but more often they shaped the metal into rods or bars. Even metal rods and bars were not very convenient. Sometimes, they were too heavy to carry around. Also, they were not uniform in size. Thus, each one had to be weighed individually to determine its value.

It soon became apparent that some of these inconveniences could be eliminated by creating metal coins of uniform size and weight and of specified value or denomination. Historians believe that state coinage originated in Lydia (an ancient kingdom that occupied the southwestern portion of what is now Turkey) during the seventh century B.C. and quickly spread throughout the ancient Mediterranean world.

The Greeks were experts at making coins; and by the year 330 B.C., they were producing coins in large numbers under the direction of Alexander the Great. The first Roman denarius was issued in the third century B.C. The influence of Roman coinage spread throughout Europe when Roman soldiers carried their coins to the countries they had conquered. Before long, many nations were producing copper, gold, or silver money.

Though coins were convenient to use and carry, they created a whole range of new temptations. For example, early coins were not perfectly round, and larcenous persons could easily shave or clip bits of precious metal from their edges. To discourage this form of defacement, coins were produced with milled edges so that changes in their edges could be easily detected. Criminals were also tempted to manufacture fake money or to artificially increase the apparent value of copper or lead coins by coating them with thin layers of silver. In some societies, these crimes of counterfeiting became so widespread and serious that convicted counterfeiters were put to death.

Activity

CO AP Do some research to learn more about the different types of coins that have been used throughout history. Create a poster on which you show pictures of five different coins, describe the time in which they were manufactured, and give their approximate value or buying power.

Name _____

Create a Coin

AP Throughout history, coins have been designed to commemorate important events and decorated in a variety of ways. For example, they have carried pictures of mythological creatures, emperors, kings, presidents, animals, and symbols. The words on their surfaces have identified the country in which they were made, defined their assigned value, and expressed significant sentiments.

Choose an imaginary place or an important event. In the space below, design a set of coins to be used in this place or to commemorate this event. Draw and label both sides of each coin. Beside each coin, write its name and value.

Paper Money

Although gold and silver coins were easier to carry than chickens, cows, or grain, large numbers of them were heavy, and carting them from place to place proved to be a nuisance. For this reason, paper notes were manufactured to represent coins. The Chinese printed the first paper money around A.D. 1200. Printed on paper made from mulberry tree bark, these early bills measured nine inches by twelve inches. Paper money quickly became popular because it was easy to carry and use.

The American colonial government first issued paper money during the Revolutionary War. These bills, called **continental currency,** lost their value because too many were printed. The phrase "not worth a continental" was frequently used at that time to describe anything that was utterly worthless.

The first official United States paper money was printed in 1861. These bills were called **greenbacks** because of the color of the ink that was used to print them. Large numbers of green-

backs were printed because the government needed money to finance the Civil War. By 1864, the greenback dollar was worth only thirty-nine cents in gold value. In 1879, the U.S. Treasury was able to acquire enough gold to restore greenbacks to full buying power.

Today, paper money, or **currency**, as it is called, is more important than coins. In the United States, currency is designed and printed by the Treasury Department's Bureau of Engraving and Printing. This "paper" money is 75 percent cotton and 25 percent linen. Each bill is printed as part of a large sheet of thirty-two bills and is given its own serial number. After these sheets are inspected, they are cut; and the resulting individual bills are put into circulation.

The average one-dollar bill remains in circulation for about eighteen months and can be folded as many as four thousand times before it finally wears out. Worn-out bills are destroyed by the twelve Federal Reserve Banks. Every working day, each one of these banks burns about $5 million in worn-out currency.

Activities

KN 1. In 1984, the U.S. Treasury Department estimated that there were 3,559,494,891 one-dollar bills in circulation. Look in an almanac or other similar reference book to determine the number of one-dollar bills that were in circulation last year.

KN
CO 2. Do some research to learn more about the coins and currencies of other periods and places. For example, you might look through a coin collector's catalog or encyclopedia, or you might visit a coin shop.

CO
AP 3. Share what you learned in activity 2 by creating a poster or chart on which you include drawings or photocopies of coins and bills and their histories and descriptions.

Name _____

Design a Dollar

AP First, look at U.S. currency and, if possible, at paper money from several other countries. Then, in the spaces below, design a dollar or some other similar bill. Remember to draw both sides of your bill and to include in your design the value of the bill, the date of its issue, the name of the country issuing it, the conditions governing its use or redemption, and any other information you think useful or pertinent.

Name _____

Coming to Terms with Money

All of the eighty terms listed below have something to do with economics, finance, and/or money. Choose twenty of these terms. Write each one of the terms you have chosen on one side of a three-inch-by-five-inch index card. Look up the definitions of these twenty terms and print them on the backs of the cards. If you have already started a pocket dictionary of economic terms (page 79, activity 1), add these cards to it. If not, alphabetize these cards, put a rubber band around them, and keep them as the beginning of a pocket dictionary of economic terms. Create new cards as you encounter additional unfamiliar terms.

bank note	estate	penny pinch
bankrupt	exchange	pennyweight
bargain	farthing	penny-wise
barter	financial	philanthropist
benefactor	fiscal	poverty
beneficiary	gain	price
bill	goods	producers
bond	greenback	profit
booty	heir	prosperity
bourse	hoard	revenue
bread	income	save
buck	inflation	scarcity
cash	interest	security
cheapskate	invest	services
commodities	investment	spend
consumers	loss	specialize
continental	lucre	squander
counterfeit	medium of exchange	stock
credit	millionaire	store of value
currency	mint	swap
debit	miser	tender
depression	monetary	trade
discount	needs	treasure
dough	numismatist	value
economical	pauper	wampum
economics	penny ante	wants
economy		wealth

greenback
numismatist
depression
philanthropist

pennyweight
monetary
cheapskate
counterfeit

Name _____

American Economic Values

Economic values are the philosophies on which an economic system is based and/or the goals that system seeks to achieve. For example, the American people want an economy that is relatively stable and secure, one that is able to provide a job for every person who wants to work. They also want a high standard of living so that their country will be a pleasant place in which to live.

Many Americans believe that the best way to achieve these goals is to allow the economy to operate as Adam Smith prescribed. They share Smith's view that the desire of producers to make a profit will cause them to work hard to make their product or service the best and that the natural competition among producers of similar products and providers of comparable services will force them to keep prices down.

For these reasons, in the United States, producers are free to decide what goods and services they will offer and what prices they will charge for them. Likewise, consumers are free to spend their money in any way they wish. There are no laws compelling consumers to spend wisely and no regulations requiring producers to make a certain number of specified products or to limit their services. To protect the buying public, laws have been passed requiring some producers to obtain licenses authorizing them to provide particular kinds of services, and producers can be held liable for products that prove unsafe or unhealthful, or for using a manufacturing process that pollutes the environment.

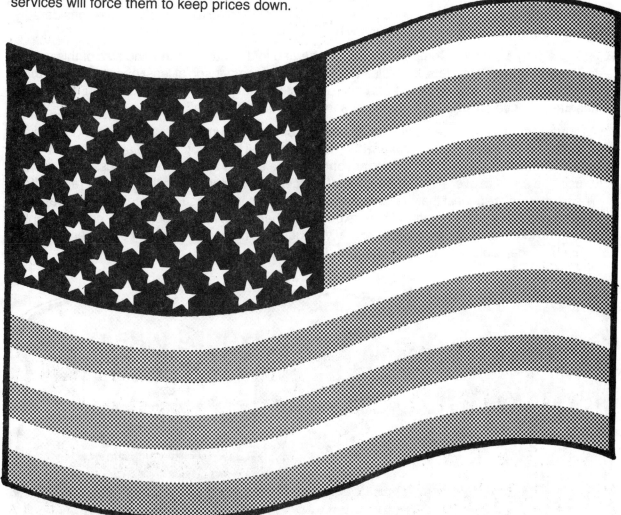

Name _____

American Economic Values Activity Sheet

KN
CO
1. Do some research to learn more about regulations designed to protect the health and safety of consumers. Select one type of product, such as automobiles, sports equipment, or toys, and learn which organized groups are concerned about the safety of these products, what legislation has been passed to protect people who buy and use these products, and which government agencies monitor the quality of these products.

KN
CO
2. Make a list of at least ten service providers who must be licensed. For example, you might include bus drivers, cosmetologists, and physicians.

KN
CO
3. Select one of the services you listed in activity 2. Do some research to learn what training the provider of this service must have to obtain a license, what tests he or she must pass, and under what circumstances the license can be revoked.

KN
CO
4. Choose a product, such as bread, laundry detergent, or gasoline. Survey grocery shelves, newspaper advertisements, or service station signs to find out what prices are being charged for this product by five to ten different producers. Share the results of your survey by means of a chart or graph.

KN
CO
AP
AN
5. Select a single product and record the price advertised for this product by one grocery store or supermarket every day for an entire month. Use these prices to construct a chart or graph. During the period in question, was the price of this product relatively stable or did it fluctuate considerably? What factors might account for this stability or fluctuation?

AN
SY
6. Select a single product. Compare the prices charged for the same brand and size of this product by five different retail outlets. If possible, include in your comparison at least one small store that is individually owned and operated and one large store that is part of a major chain. If there are substantial price differences, what factors might account for them?

AP
AN
SY
EV
7. Although no effort has been made in the past to compel consumers to spend their money wisely, some observers have noted with alarm the rise in personal bankruptcies, the apparent willingness of banks and stores to extend credit to anyone, and the equally apparent willingness of consumers to use this credit to overextend themselves financially by buying things they cannot really afford. These observers suggest that the government should regulate consumer credit in some way. First, give this problem some thought. Then, explain whether or not limiting consumer credit is consistent with American economic values. Finally, suggest a method of curbing consumer credit that might be acceptable to both consumers and producers.

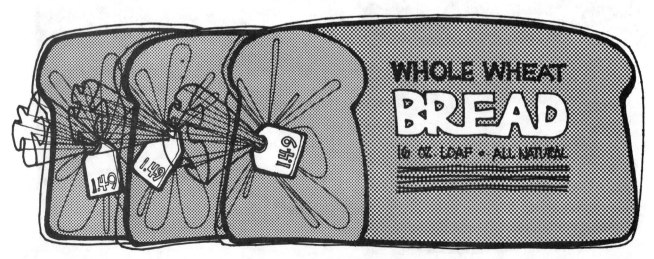

Name _____

Economic Systems

A **system** is an organized social situation or framework. Thus, an **economic system** is the organization that is imposed on an economy, the framework within which the economy operates, or the form the economy takes. The system is determined by both the philosophy that guides the economy and the regulations that govern it. There are three basic types of economic systems: the free enterprise economic system, the socialist economic system, and the communist economic system.

The **free enterprise economic system,** which is also called **private enterprise, capitalism,** or a **pure market system,** was supported by Scottish economist Adam Smith (1723–1790) in his study entitled *Inquiry into the Nature and Causes of the Wealth of Nations.* In this study, which was published in 1776, Smith described the intricate interrelationships among money, prices, wages, and division of labor. He advocated a natural liberty of trade and commerce, which he said would produce the greatest wealth. Because Smith believed economies should be driven by self-interest and would be regulated by competition, he asserted that governments should not attempt to regulate them or to interfere in any way with the natural course of their operation. Smith's ideas strongly influenced both the economic and the political thinking of his day and are still cited by present-day supporters of the free enterprise system. This system is the one that operates in the United States and Canada and in many other countries where resources are privately owned, producers are free to make and sell what they wish, consumers are free to buy and use what they wish, and government planning, control, and intervention are minimal.

The **socialist economic system** is characterized by far more government planning and control than the free enterprise system. Under socialism, the government owns and operates most or all of the large industries, such as coal mines, railroads, steel mills, and television networks. Thus, the government establishes the labor, wage, and employee benefit policies for these industries. Workers are free to protest policies they do not like; but if they quit one job because of a basic disagreement with their employer and seek another position within the same industry, they may find that taking a new job means working for the same old boss—the government.

Socialist countries usually have comprehensive systems of financial aid to pay workers' medical bills and to provide for them in their old age. Taxes in socialist countries are usually high because of the heavy welfare burden socialist programs place on government treasuries. Examples of socialist economic systems can be seen in Great Britain, India, Norway, and Sweden.

Economic Systems
(continued)

The **communist economic system,** which is also termed a **command economy,** is one in which the government owns all, or almost all, of the means of production. Under this system, the government not only owns the farms and factories in which food is grown and goods are made but also owns the markets and stores in which these products are sold. Thus, the government controls both wages paid for work and prices paid for goods. While consumers are free to spend their money as they wish, their choice of goods and services is limited to what the government decides to make available. China and the Soviet Union are communist countries.

The communist economic system was described by a German political philosopher named Karl Marx (1818–1883). Working with Friedrich Engels, Marx wrote a treatise called *The Communist Manifesto.* In this treatise, Marx and Engels interpreted history as a continuing class struggle between employers and workers. They described their belief that the free enterprise system would lead to increasingly severe economic depressions during which large numbers of workers would lose their jobs. The cumulative result of these depressions would be extreme discontent among workers, who would eventually lead a revolution to replace the free enterprise economic system with a communist one. Concluding that the accumulation of wealth by one group of people in an economy (the upper classes) would result in the accumulation of misery for another group (the workers or masses), Marx and Engels called upon workers of the world to unite in an effort to throw off their chains.

Very few functioning economic systems are pure examples of any one of these three types. Instead, most of them are mixed systems in which elements from at least two of these basic types are combined. For example, in the United States, a free enterprise economy, the government plays an active role in promoting economic stability and growth by raising or lowering interest rates, increasing or decreasing the money supply, and changing the tax laws. On the other hand, while the Soviet Union is a communist economic system, it responds to some extent to market-determined prices and allows some kinds of private ownership. The Swedish economy, which is classified as socialist, is also a mixed system. Although the government is deeply involved in achieving economic stability and redistributing income, it actually owns less than 10 percent of all business.

Economic Systems Activity Sheet

**AN
SY** 1. Do some research to learn more about the three basic types of economic systems. Then make a chart or table in which you list the different characteristics of these systems and also list the advantages and disadvantages of each one.

**AP
AN** 2. As a well-known economist, you have been commissioned to design an economic system that will be financially successful and will benefit its citizens. You can use aspects of well-known economic systems and/or create your own. What will you call your system? How will it operate? Whom will it benefit? In what ways?

**KN
CO** 3. The United States economy is a free enterprise economic system, yet the United States government sometimes interferes in the economy to preserve, encourage, or protect particular industries. The means that the government uses for doing so include loan guarantees, subsidies, tariffs, and special tax levies or tax breaks. Do some research to learn more about government intervention in some particular area of the economy, such as agriculture, energy, or transportation. Share what you learn by means of a brief report.

Name _____

Federal Income Tax

The United States and many other countries require citizens to pay a tax on their income. Each year, wage earners must file with an agency of the government forms on which they report the amount of their annual income. They are then required to pay to the government a sum of money which is a certain percentage of this income.

In the United States and some other countries, the income tax is **progressive**. The same rate, or percent, is not used to figure tax for everyone. Instead, the percentage progresses, or gets larger, as the amount of income increases. For example, in 1985, a single person whose annual

income was $11,000 paid $1,218, or 11 percent of his annual income; and a single person whose annual income was $22,000 paid $3,651, or 16.5 percent of his annual income.

This system has been praised as "fair" by some economists because it makes the financial burden of running the country fall most heavily on those who are most able to pay. This system has been criticized as "socialistic" by other economists who view it as unwanted and unwarranted government intervention in the economy and as an attempt to redistribute wealth.

Activities

KN
CO
1. Obtain a copy of the federal tax table that is used to determine individual income tax. Select an annual income and locate the tax that would be paid by a single person with that income and by a married couple with that combined income.

CO
AP
2. Select a series of incomes and use a line graph to represent the change in amount owed with income earned.

CO
AP
3. Use a line or bar graph to represent the change in percent of income paid as income increases.

AN
SY
EV
4. Do you think that the progressive income tax is fair? Why or why not?

Name _____

The Market System

In any economy, some system must be used to decide what products should be produced, how they should be produced, and who should have access to them. One way these decisions are made is by means of markets. A **market** is the place or atmosphere in which goods are sold or exchanged, or the mechanism by which this exchange is accomplished. A market can be as simple as the place where a farmer sells fresh produce to a housewife or as complex as the place where brokers buy and sell corporate stocks for client-investors.

If left unregulated, markets usually operate on the basis of supply and demand. **Supply** is the amount of a product or service that producers want to sell. **Demand** is the amount of a product or service that consumers want to purchase.

Several factors influence supply. Among these factors are weather and transportation. For example, frost may damage orange crops, and a truck strike may mean that oranges cannot be transported far from the orchards in which they are grown.

Likewise, several factors influence demand. These factors include the price of the product itself, the prices of other products that might be substituted for it, and the prices of products that must be used with it. For example, a substantial increase in bus fare or a substantial decrease in the cost of gasoline may increase the demand for automobiles.

The Market System Activity Sheet

CO
AP

1. Choose one type of product that seems to be in demand in your area. Check advertising fliers, newspaper and magazine advertisements, and television commercials to discover the ways in which advertisers are promoting this product.

AP
AN

2. Another factor that affects the demand for a product is the location in which it is being sold. For example, in a cold, wet climate where there is frequent snow, the demand for skiis, sleds, and snowmobiles will be much greater than it is in a warm, dry area, where snow is infrequent. Consider how the weather affects supply and demand in your area. Write a paragraph in which you describe one specific example.

AN

3. Select a product that you would expect to have seasonal appeal. For example, you might consider ice cream cones, pizza, or swim suits. Call or visit a store that sells this product and ask about the monthly sales volume. Use a line graph to illustrate how demand for this product varies with season. If there is less variation than you had expected, do some additional research to learn what producers (and their advertising agencies) do to increase demand during the off-season.

AN
SY
EV

4. The markets of the Middle Ages were controlled by the guild merchants. Today, many markets are uncontrolled. Producers selling in these markets are free to offer any product or service at any price, and consumers buying in these markets are free to purchase any offered product or service they wish and can afford. Under this system, are producers and consumers entirely free to make their own decisions or are the members of each group controlled to a certain extent by the members of the other group? For example, what happens if a producer offers a product or service that no one wants to buy? And what happens if a consumer wants to buy a product or service that no producer is offering? Think about these problems and describe at least one thing a producer might do to generate demand for an unwanted product and at least one thing a creative consumer might do if a desired product or service does not exist or is not available.

Competition

Adam Smith's well-known study entitled *Inquiry into the Nature and Causes of the Wealth of Nations* was published in 1776. In this study, Smith called for a natural liberty of trade and commerce, which he said would be driven by self-interest and regulated by competition. **Competition** is the name given to the efforts of two or more producers *acting independently* to secure the business or patronage of consumers on the basis or quality, price, and/or special features. Smith believed that competition would "regulate commerce" by forcing producers to make the best goods possible and to sell them at the lowest prices consistent with making a profit.

The problem with Smith's theory is that there are imperfections in the system. Sometimes there is only one producer of a product or one provider of a service; therefore, no real competition is possible. This situation is called a **monopoly.**

Sometimes, different producers of the same product agree among themselves to charge the same price for their goods. Making such an agreement is called **price fixing.** Although there are laws against price fixing, violations of these laws are often difficult to prove and prosecute.

Sometimes, established producers of a product use price wars, rights buyouts, and other similar tactics to force newer competitors out of the market. A **price war** is a period of intense commercial competition in which producers repeatedly cut prices in an attempt to charge less than their competitors. In such a war, prices are often lowered below cost. With no profit, smaller companies are unable to pay their bills and become casualties of the war. After these companies go out of business, prices are raised back to their previous levels or even higher to recoup "war" losses. In a **rights buyout,** an established company buys the rights to produce a product originated by another company and perceived as potential competition. The company purchasing the rights may then produce the product or simply hold it off the market. In either event, competition is severely curtailed or eliminated entirely.

Competition Activity Sheet

KN
CO
AP

1. One problem with allowing competition to regulate commerce is that producers may become overly cost-conscious and not give adequate attention to product quality or consumer safety. This problem was particularly evident in the United States automobile industry during the 1950s and 1960s and was documented by consumer advocate Ralph Nader in a book entitled *Unsafe at Any Speed.* The work of Nader and others forced congress to take a look at the ability of American-made automobiles to be driven safely and to protect the passengers within them in the event of an accident. As a result, legislation was passed, agencies were established, inspections were initiated, models that proved faulty were recalled for repair, automakers were forced to give more attention to purchaser satisfaction and passenger safety, and consumers became more aware. Do some research to learn more about features that have been added to automobiles over the years to make them safer and more comfortable. Share what you learn by means of an **Auto Improvements Time Line.**

KN
CO
AP
AN
SY

2. Sometimes government regulations limit competition. For example, for many years, the U.S. government regulated the routes flown and the fares charged in the airline industry. When this industry was **deregulated** during the 1980s, the immediate result was more flights and cheaper fares; but some less-traveled flights and routes were eliminated altogether. Passengers were pleased about the lower fares but not so pleased about the inconvenience of being unable to fly nonstop and of having to follow less direct routes to their destinations. Do some research to learn what routes were flown by two major U.S. airline companies before deregulation and after deregulation. Draw these routes on a map of the United States and compare them. Along which air corridors was service increased? Along which air corridors was service decreased? Were these changes probably influenced in part by supply and demand? Explain your answer.

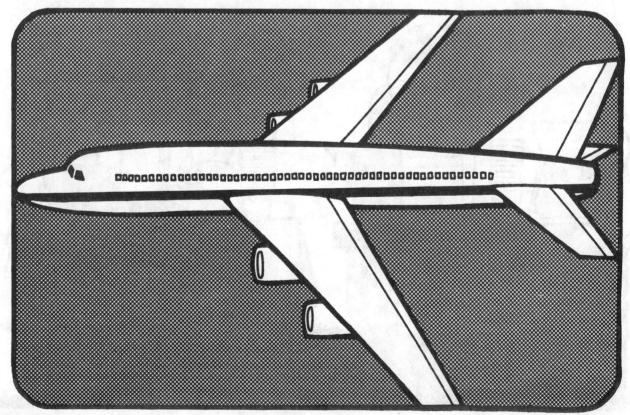

Name _____

Regulations—Good or Bad?

Automobile drivers need to know that the brakes on their cars are safe. People eating in restaurants need to feel confident that the food they are being served has been prepared under sanitary conditions. People who are sick want to be able to take their medicine without the fear of unexpected or harmful side effects. Consumers want quality and safety, but producers want profit. Sometimes, these two wants are in conflict. For this reason, the government passes laws and establishes standards for safety and performance.

Government regulation of products and services is a relatively new development. As recently as eighty years ago, regulations of this type were rare. For example, at the turn of the century, meat inspection was unheard of. In 1906, a novel by Upton Sinclair (1878–1968) called *The Jungle* was published. This novel painted a grim picture of life in the Chicago stockyards and of the nation's meatpacking industry. Today, nearly forty-one thousand regulations control every fast-food hamburger that is sold. These regulations set standards for everything from the percentage of real meat a "beef" patty must contain to the amount of pesticide it can contain.

Economists debate whether regulations help or hurt the free enterprise system. Critics feel that complying with unnecessary regulations costs businesses valuable time and money. They point out that the money required to meet government standards cannot be used to buy new equipment or to improve the product. They also argue that regulations reduce competition and keep the economy from operating at peak efficiency. Regulation advocates argue that government rules force an industry to face and solve problems, thus making it become more creative and helping it be more productive.

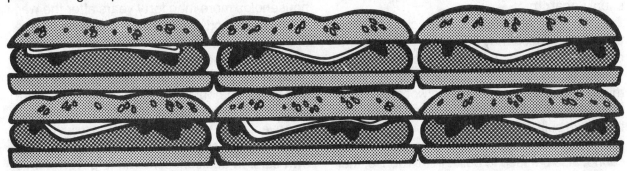

Activities

KN CO AP
1. Do some research to learn more about government regulation of products and services. Share what you learn by means of a time line on which you give dates and descriptions of milestone legislation.

KN CO AP
2. Make a chart on which you list the names, mailing addresses, and telephone numbers of at least ten government agencies established to protect consumers and/or to respond to their complaints.

AP AN
3. If you have been dissatisfied with a product or a service, write a letter of complaint to one of the agencies listed on your chart.

AP AN EV
4. Upton Sinclair's novel *The Jungle* called public and congressional attention to the need for stricter regulations within the meatpacking industry. Ralph Nader's *Unsafe at Any Speed* did the same for the automobile industry, and Rachel Carson's *Silent Spring* called attention to the dangers inherent in the uncontrolled use of pesticides within the food-growing industry and elsewhere. Make a chart on which you list the author, title, and year of publication for ten books that have increased public awareness of a problem and resulted in legislation. What does your chart suggest about the power of the pen?

Name _____

Scarcity and Choices

Resources are the computable wealth, the raw materials, or the available means of manufacturing a product or providing a service. Economists classify resources into three basic categories: human resources, natural resources, and capital resources. **Human resources** are people and their physical and mental energy. **Natural resources** are the raw materials from which products are made. They include animals, plants, minerals, clean air, fertile soil, and fresh water. **Capital resources** are the tools and machines needed to make products and the factories and office buildings in which products are made and companies are managed.

Although the worldwide supply of resources is vast, it is not infinite. Each resource exists only in limited amount. At certain times and in specific places, some resources are in very short supply. Economists call the condition, quality, or state of existing only in limited amount or being in short supply **scarcity.**

Scarcity forces people to make choices about the ways in which they use their resources. For example, knowing that, at any one time, the supply of wood is limited, people using wood must choose between using the wood they have to build houses and using it to warm the houses they have built. Whatever their choice, they must remember that wood burned to provide warmth cannot also be used to build. In this sense, their choices are **mutually exclusive,** and their decision is **irreversible.**

One way people deal with scarcity is by **allocating resources.** That is, they decide that a certain amount of the resources available will be set aside to be used in specific ways. For example, the people with the wood might allocate some types or amounts of it to building and other types or amounts to burning. They might express these allocations as percentages of the total amount of usable wood produced within a specified period of time.

Another way people deal with scarcity is by using one resource instead of another. This process is called **substituting,** and the alternate resources are called **substitutes.** In the example above, people might decide to use stone instead of wood for building or to use coal instead of wood for burning.

During World War II, a large percentage of the available dairy products was allocated to feed members of the U.S. armed forces. As a result, certain ones of these products became scarce in civilian markets. When the supply of butter became too small to meet the demand, creative producers used vegetable oils and other ingredients to make margarine. This wartime substitute for butter is still being used in many households more than forty years after the war.

The energy crisis of 1973 is a graphic example of the problems associated with scarcity. In that year oil became very scarce. As a result, the price of gasoline rose dramatically, and people had to spend hours in long lines at service stations just to fill their tanks. To lessen the cost and inconvenience, some people chose to walk or to use public transportation instead of driving their own cars. In addition, some state governments established an allocation system under which license plate numbers were used to determine when car owners could fill up. People with odd-numbered plates could buy on Monday, Wednesday, and Friday. People with even-numbered plates could buy on Tuesday, Thursday, and Saturday. Many service stations were closed on Sunday.

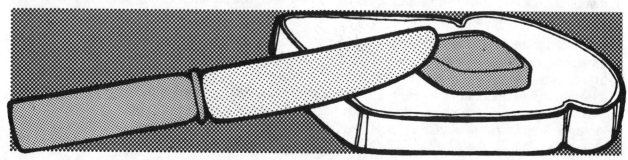

Scarcity and Choices Activity Sheet

KN
CO
1. Do some research to learn more about periods in which specific resources have been scarce because of natural disaster, weather, war, or unusually heavy demand. Represent what you learn on a scarcity time line.

KN
CO
AP
2. Divide a sheet of paper into three columns. Label the columns **Human Resources, Natural Resources,** and **Capital Resources.** See how many resources you can list within each column.

KN
CO
3. An old Latin saying proclaims *Mater artium necessitas,* which means "Necessity is the mother of invention." Throughout history, when people have experienced shortages of things they have needed, they have invented new products or discovered new ways to use old products to meet their needs. For example, during World War II, margarine was developed as a substitute for butter, and ways were found to use nylon as a substitute for silk (in stockings) and for rubber (in tires). Do some research to learn more about these and other inventions that were born of necessity.

AN
SY
EV
4. When categorizing resources, some economists recognize a fourth type—time. In this context, time is the number of hours available for producing a product or providing a service. Other economists argue that, because the work people do is measured in manhours, time and people are actually the same resource, that time to do a job is meaningless without people to do the work. What do you think? Is time a separate resource? Explain your answer.

AP
AN
5. During the energy crisis of 1973, the supply of gasoline was unevenly distributed throughout the United States. Some states had supplies that were more than sufficient to meet the needs of their residents, while other states had inadequate supplies and suffered real shortages. Offer some possible reasons for this problem and then propose at least one way of allocating a scarce resource, such as gasoline, so that the supply in any one place is more nearly equal to the demand in that place.

AN
EV
6. During the energy crisis of 1973, the people in some special groups were exempt from the gasoline purchase limitations imposed on the members of other groups. For example, the owners or drivers of certain farm and food delivery vehicles were exempt from the strict limitations imposed on the drivers of passenger vehicles. Do you think exemptions of this kind are necessary? Do you think they are fair? Explain your answers.

The Potlatch

Every culture that values economic power has a way of showing off that power. In some cultures, the means of displaying economic power is a fancy car and a power watch. In other cultures, it is a large estate and many servants. In still other cultures, it is having many wives or owning many animals. Perhaps no means of displaying economic power is stranger or has attracted more attention than that used by Kwakiutl and related Indian tribes of the Pacific Northwest.

The Kwakiutl Indians are a group of closely related North American Indian tribes who inhabit Vancouver Island and the adjacent mainland of British Columbia in Canada. They display economic power by publicly disposing of wealth. Their means for doing so is an elaborate ceremony called a **potlatch.**

The potlatch is a winter ceremony which usually lasts several days and is characterized by boasting, feasting, and dancing. As a part of this ceremony, the host gives expensive gifts to certain ones of his guests. These gifts are usually copper plates and goat's hair blankets. In return, his guests acknowledge his great wealth and show him the respect his economic success has earned.

But the story does not end there. It is Kwakiutl custom that those who receive gifts are obligated to honor their host by entertaining him under equally lavish circumstances and by presenting him with even more expensive gifts. Thus, a clever Kwakiutl chief or man of wealth can use the potlatch to enrich himself. In similar manner, a group of disgruntled braves can use the potlatch to impoverish a disliked chief or tribe member.

Activities

CO AP AN   1. The signs of economic power, or status, vary from one culture to another. Select three cultures other than your own. Do some research to discover what signs are used to display economic power within each of these cultures. Share what you learn by means of a table or chart.

CO AP AN   2. Examine the broad culture of which you are a part. List the signs that are used by the members of this culture to display their economic power.

CO AP AN   3. Examine the subculture, or peer group, of which you are a part. List the signs that are used by the members of this subculture to display their economic power, or status.

SY   4. Compare the signs you listed in activity 2 or 3 with the Kwakiutl means of displaying economic power. In what ways are they similar? In what ways are they different?

EV   5. Consider the Kwakiutl potlatch from an economic point of view. Was the lavish gift-giving that was a part of this ceremony a wise use of resources? Explain your answer.

Name _____

Inflation

The English word **inflate** means "to enlarge by filling with air or some other gas." It is this meaning that you have in mind when you talk about inflating a balloon. The word inflate also means "to expand or increase abnormally or unwisely," and it is this meaning that economists have in mind when they talk about an inflationary economy. **Inflation** is a period in which the prices charged for goods and services rise, and the economy expands abnormally or unwisely. A certain percentage of increase in prices is thought by economists to be normal, but they term excessive increases **inflationary** and view them with alarm.

Economists distinguish between at least two types of inflation on the basis of what appears to cause, or drive, them. One of these types is **cost-push inflation.** In cost-push inflation, the cost of making goods and of providing services rises, producers increase their prices, workers demand higher wages, and the cost of making goods and providing services rises again. As you can see, inflation of this type can become an unending cycle of higher costs, higher prices, higher wages, and higher costs once again.

The other of these types of inflation is termed **demand-pull.** During periods of demand-pull inflation, consumers have plenty of money to spend, but too few goods and services are available to meet their demands. In this situation, goods and services appear to be underpriced, and producers raise prices until a buying slow-down signals that rising costs have decreased demand.

Inflation is not all bad or, maybe one should say, not equally bad for everyone. A small and steady amount of inflation is viewed by some economists as unavoidable and the surest indication of an active and expanding economy. Also, inflation increases the value of certain assets, such as houses. For example, if you buy a house and the cost of building houses goes up, then the price of the house you own rises with it. In this way, the equity in your house increases, and you are better off financially during or after the inflation than you were before.

Another cost that is affected by inflation is the cost of borrowing money. When you borrow money from a bank, the bank charges interest. **Interest** is rent charged or paid for the temporary use of someone else's money. Because interest rates go up during periods of inflation, borrowing at these times will cost more than it would normally. The other side of the coin is that, if you have money to invest—to let a bank or other lending institution borrow—you will receive more interest from the bank or institution for the use of your money.

The people who suffer most during periods of inflation are those who are living on fixed incomes and who do not hold any assets or have any investments that act as a protection, or **hedge,** against inflation. Most of these people are older retired workers who find that their monthly pension checks buy fewer and fewer of the things they want and need.

Activity

CO AP AN SY
Make a list of ten items you buy regularly. For example, your list might include admission to a movie, a box of crayons, a comic book, an ice cream cone, a package of notebook paper, a pack of gum, a pencil, and a tablet. Beside each item, write the price you usually pay for it. Then ask your parents to tell you what they paid for these ten items when they were your age. Record their prices beside yours. If possible, ask your grandparents to tell you what they paid for these same items when they were your age. Record their prices beside your parents'. Compare these prices. For which items have prices increased the least? For which items have prices increased the most? What factors might account for these increases? What is the average rate of inflation over the period you have documented for the particular items on your list? How does this rate compare with the actual rate of inflation over the same period of time?

Name _____

Depression

The English word **depression** is used to designate a period of reduced activity. An **economic depression** is a period of slowed economic activity in which there are more goods and services on the market than consumers want to buy, prices fall, producers close plants and lay off workers to cut costs, and unemployment increases.

Depressions often follow periods of inflation. The rising interest rates that accompany an inflation eventually cause consumers to curtail credit buying. As a result, the demand for large appliances, automobiles, homes, and other products that are paid for over time drops. If depressions are mild and temporary, they are viewed by some economists as the normal way in which an inflated market economy corrects itself.

Economists sometimes differentiate among depressions according to how deep they are (the **degree**) and how long they last (the **duration**). For example, they use the word **slumps** to refer to dips in economic activity that are slight and temporary, use the word **recessions** to refer to drops in economic activity that are more severe and longer lasting, and almost never use the word **depression** except in reference to the Great Depression of the 1930s.

The Great Depression followed the Stock Market Crash of 1929. To understand the Great Depression, you need to know something about the stock market. Corporations borrow money to buy new machines and to make new products by selling **stocks.** People who buy these stocks are called **stockholders,** or **investors.** In return for the money they invest, they are given ownership of a small part of the total corporation. Each part is called a **share.** The number of shares an investor owns is indicated on a piece of paper called a **stock certificate.** If the value of the corporation rises, so does the value of each share. If the value of the corporation falls, so does the value of each share. Wise investors try to buy when stock prices are low and to sell when these prices are high. By doing so, they can make a profit on the money they have invested.

In 1929, after a decade of unprecedented growth and unhealthy speculation, the prices of corporate stocks plunged precipitously. As a result, shares in some corporations were worth less than the paper on which their stock certificates were printed. Investors lost the money they had invested, and corporations went bankrupt. Eighty-five thousand businesses closed their doors forever. More than 15 million workers were unemployed. Many of them stood in long lines in cities for free soup or roamed the countryside in search of work.

The Great Depression lasted ten years. During this time, both producers and consumers lost faith in the U.S. economic system. As one solution, President Franklin D. Roosevelt and other government officials sought to buttress the country's sagging economy by providing jobs for the unemployed. They established huge public works projects in which people were hired to build dams, clean up parks, and to build, restore, or beautify public buildings. Despite these efforts, it was not until World War II that the economy finally recovered and prosperity returned.

Activity

During 1986, the per-barrel price of crude oil dropped from $27 to below $15 and threatened to go as low as $10. The good news was that this price drop brought immediate cuts in the price of gasoline, heating oil, and diesel fuel. Less immediate but equally welcome were cuts in the prices of petroleum-based products ranging from pesticides to carpet fibers. The bad news was that the bottom dropped out of the economies in oil-producing states like Louisiana, Oklahoma, Texas, and Wyoming. Businesses closed, banks failed, and workers were unemployed. In Texas, for example, each $1 per-barrel drop in oil prices meant a loss of 25,000 jobs. Make a good news/bad news chart on which you list the items for which prices should go down as the result of a drop in oil prices, the groups of people who would receive economic benefit from these lower prices, and the groups of people who would suffer economic loss as a result of these lower prices.

Name _____

Urban Economic Problems

In the year 1800, only 6 percent of the population in the United States lived in towns. The other 94 percent lived on farms and in the countryside. By the year 2000, 85 percent of the population will live in towns or cities, and only 15 percent will reside in rural areas. As a result of this dramatic population shift, U.S. cities are facing some serious economic questions: Will there be enough clean air, fresh water, affordable housing, and available transportation to make city living tolerable? Who will bear the costs for the repairs and improvements that are sorely needed?

Some newer cities have been carefully planned, but most older cities have grown in a haphazard fashion with little thought being given to commercial requirements, housing needs, traffic flow, and parking patterns. Commercial and industrial buildings are often not located near transportation facilities. Low-cost housing is hard to find and situated many miles from employment sites. Public transportation has not kept pace with the demand for it, and facilities for private transportation are inadequate. Many of today's busy highways were yesterday's byways. Built for the meandering gait of horse-drawn buggies and carts, they are ill-suited for more modern, faster-moving vehicles.

The cores of many older cities are deteriorating. High taxes, high land values, high rents, and substandard conditions have driven many businesses and industries to the suburbs. In some places, office and apartment buildings stand vacant and fall victim to vandals who spray messages on the walls and break the remaining windows. This condition is called **urban blight.**

Economists and city planners often work together to rebuild decaying cities. In some instances, waterfront warehouses and abandoned factories have been converted into apartments, studios, shops, and restaurants. In other cities, crowded tenements have been razed and replaced by housing projects that include recreational spaces as well as living quarters. This process is called **urban renewal.** It is controversial because sometimes the poor tenants, who are evicted from the buildings while they are being renovated, are unable to afford the higher rents that are charged after the remodeling has taken place.

Urban problems are easy to list, and solutions for some of them seem obvious—build housing and parking structures, widen streets, provide inexpensive public transportation, pipe in water—but the economic question remains: Who bears the costs and pays the bill?

Activities

KN 1. If you live in a town or city, survey your parents or other adults regarding the problems it is facing. List at least five.

CO
AP
AN 2. Select one of the problems you listed in activity 1 and offer a solution for it. Include diagrams, drawings, and detailed descriptions in your solution.

CO
AN 3. Estimate the cost of the solution you have proposed and explain how this cost might be borne and the bill, paid.

Name _____

Innovations and the Economy

Economists estimate that nearly one-third of all economic growth is a result of innovation. **Innovation** is the introduction of new ideas, methods, or devices. Innovation encourages economic growth by creating new products, improving old products, and making existing products less costly and more available. For example, ten years ago, it was unusual to find a computer in a home or school. Today, because innovations have made computers less costly and easier to operate, they are found in thousands of homes and schools.

Because innovations benefit the economy, economists have expressed alarm that there is less innovation today than there was ten years

ago. They cite as evidence the fact that the number of patents filed in the United States by inventors has dropped from 56,000 in 1971 to less than 33,000 in 1983. To encourage innovation, some companies have grouped their researchers into small teams and given them more freedom. These companies have also offered prizes, or bonuses, to employees who suggest effective ways to cut costs, improve existing products, or create new ones.

One company with a reputation for encouraging employee innovation is Minnesota Mining and Manufacturing, better known as 3M. Two of the products their employees have invented and/or improved are transparent tape and Post-It™ self-stick notes.

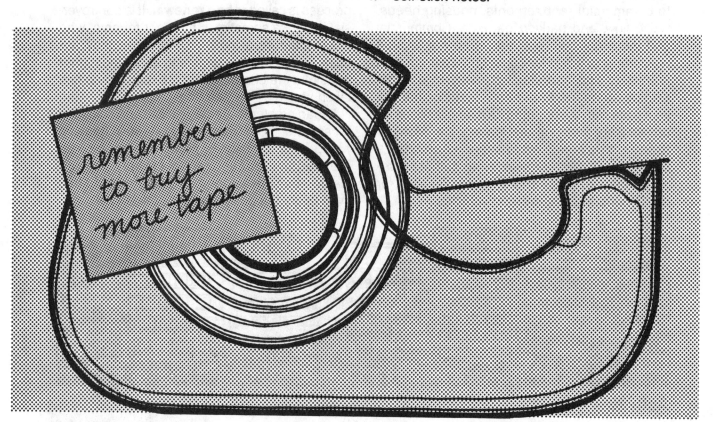

Activities

CO
AP
AN

1. Think of some things that annoy you or someone you know, like biting into a stale nut in a candy bar, trying to find a pair of eyeglasses, or getting gum stuck to the bottom of your shoe. List at least five.

CO
AN

2. Select one of the annoyances you listed in activity 1 and invent a prevention or solution. Use labeled diagrams, drawings, and words to describe your invention in detail.

Correlated Activities

KN
CO
Over the years, many economists and economic philosophers have recorded their ideas about the structure and purpose of economies and have described the ideal economic system. As is true in other areas as well, not all economists agree about what is right or fair or about how an economy should work and whom it should benefit. Choose one of the following economists and make a report to your class in which you explain his or her point of view: Irma Adelman, Martin Feldstein, Milton Friedman, John Kenneth Galbraith, John Maynard Keynes, Simon Kuznets, Arthur Laffer, Thomas Robert Malthus, Karl Marx, David Ricardo, Joseph Schumpeter, James Tobin, and Thorstein Bunde Veblen.

KN
CO
Choose one of the following economic terms and create a cartoon, chart, graph, or picture to explain its meaning: **balance of payments, bear market, bull market, gross national product, laissez-faire, social security,** and **third world.**

KN
CO
List the names of four countries in which the economy is capitalistic, four countries in which the economy is socialistic, and four countries in which the economy is communistic. Locate these countries on a world map or globe.

KN
CO
The largest gold nugget ever found was a 2,280-ounce hunk of this precious metal discovered in Australia in 1869. Do some research to learn about other gold discoveries and the gold rushes that followed them. For each one, write a paragraph in which you tell where and how the gold was discovered and describe the ways in which this discovery affected the existing economy.

KN
CO
Gold belonging to eight different nations is stored behind a ninety-ton door at Fort Knox. Do some research to learn more about Fort Knox. Where is it? What does it look like? When was it established? Who uses it? How has it changed over the years?

CO
AP
AN
Today many people use credit cards to charge some of the goods and services they purchase. When they do so, they are actually borrowing money to pay for these purchases and are temporarily postponing the outflow of their own cash. What are some of the advantages and disadvantages associated with buying on credit?

AP
AN
SY
In George Bernard Shaw's play *Pygmalion* (1913), a poor London flower girl is transformed into an elegant lady by a professor of phonetics who "corrects" her cockney speech patterns. This play was the basis for the highly successful Broadway musical entitled *My Fair Lady.* Think about the idea here. In our society, do people react differently to a rich person than they do to a poor person? Is this difference in reaction based on appearances and mannerisms—the way the person is dressed and groomed, the way the person talks and moves? Explain your answer. Where possible, give specific examples from your own experience.

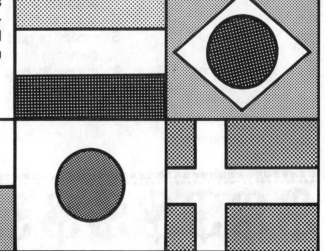

Name _____

Posttest

Match these terms with their definitions by writing the correct letter on each line.

_____ 1. barter

_____ 2. competition

_____ 3. consumer

_____ 4. credit

_____ 5. currency

_____ 6. deposit

_____ 7. depression

_____ 8. economics

_____ 9. greenback

_____ 10. inflation

_____ 11. interest

_____ 12. market

_____ 13. money

_____ 14. potlatch

_____ 15. producer

_____ 16. profit

_____ 17. reserves

_____ 18. resources

_____ 19. scarcity

_____ 20. wampum

A. the efforts of two or more producers acting independently to secure the business or patronage of consumers on the basis of quality, price, and/or special features

B. anyone who buys goods and/or services

C. a sum of money left with a goldsmith or bank for safekeeping

D. the study of how people use their resources to meet their needs and satisfy their wants

E. paper money first issued by the United States government during the Civil War

F. an amount charged or paid for borrowed money; rent charged or paid for the temporary use of someone else's money

G. a ceremonial feast common among the Kwakiutl and other Indians of the northwest coast at which the host distributed lavish gifts to show off his wealth

H. the remainder when the cost of making goods or providing services is subtracted from the price charged for them

I. available means, raw materials, or computable wealth

J. beads made from polished shells, strung in strands or belts, and used by North American Indians as money

K. to trade by exchanging one item for another; to swap without using money

L. the amount or sum a consumer is allowed to borrow at interest and/or to pay for over a period of time

M. paper money

N. a period of slowed economic activity in which there are more goods than people want, prices fall, and unemployment is high

O. a period in which there is an increase in buying power relative to available goods, and prices charged for goods and services rise

P. the place or atmosphere in which goods are sold or exchanged, or the mechanism by which this exchange is accomplished

Q. anything that is given or received in return for goods or services

R. anyone who makes goods or provides services

S. money or gold kept on hand by banks to meet the immediate demands of depositors

T. the quality or state of existing only in limited amount or being in short supply

$$$$$$$$$$$$$$

Answer Key

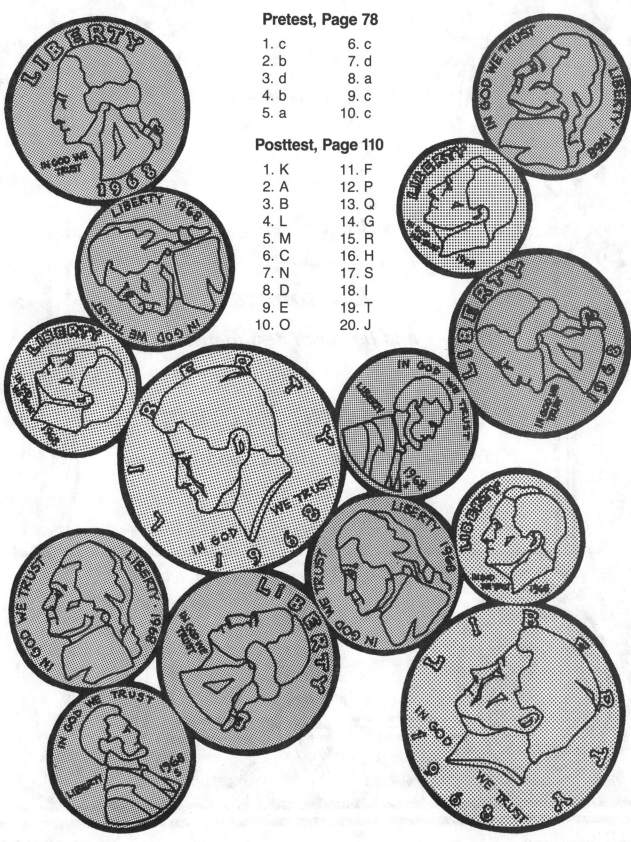

Pretest, Page 78

1. c	6. c
2. b	7. d
3. d	8. a
4. b	9. c
5. a	10. c

Posttest, Page 110

1. K	11. F
2. A	12. P
3. B	13. Q
4. L	14. G
5. M	15. R
6. C	16. H
7. N	17. S
8. D	18. I
9. E	19. T
10. O	20. J

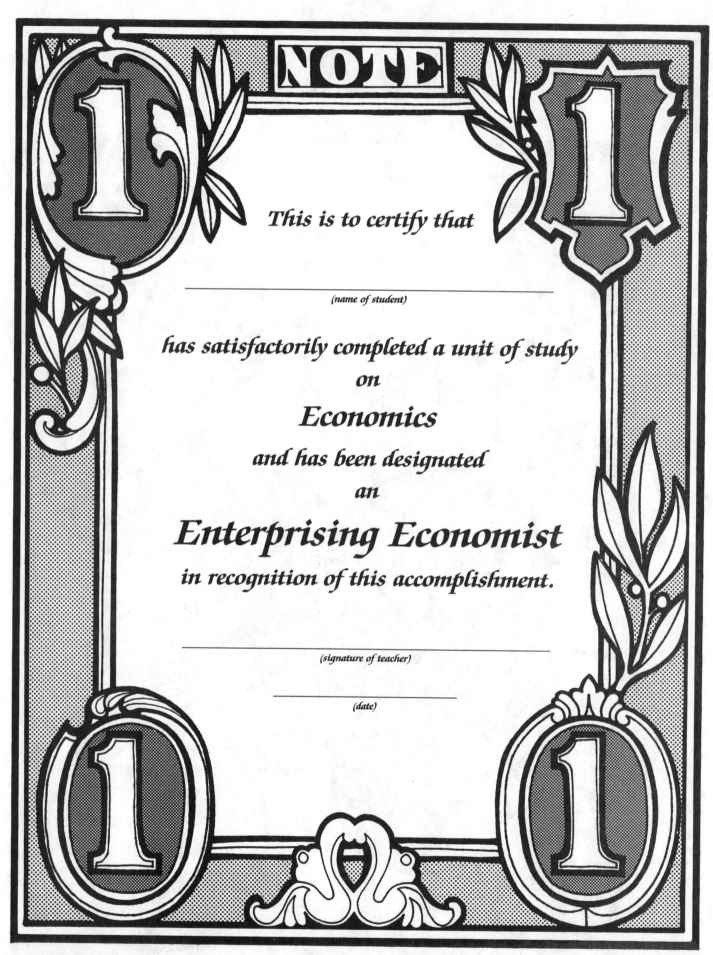

NOTE

This is to certify that

_____
(name of student)

has satisfactorily completed a unit of study
on
Economics
and has been designated
an

Enterprising Economist

in recognition of this accomplishment.

_____
(signature of teacher)

_____
(date)